Enlightenment

Shelagh Stephenson

CW00481331

Methuen Drama

Published by Methuen 2005

1 3 5 7 9 10 8 6 4 2

First published in 2005 by
Methuen Publishing Limited
215 Vauxhall Bridge Road
London SW1V 1EJ

Copyright © 2005 by Shelagh Stephenson

Shelagh Stephenson has asserted her rights under the
Copyright, Designs and Patents Act, 1988,
to be identified as the author of this work

Methuen Publishing Limited Reg. No. 3543167

A CIP catalogue record for this book is available
from the British Library

ISBN 0 413 77521 6

Typeset by Country Setting, Kingsdown, Kent
Printed and bound in Great Britain by
Cox and Wyman Ltd, Reading, Berkshire

Caution

All rights whatsoever in these plays are strictly reserved and application
for performance etc. should be made before rehearsals begin
to the author's agent: MacFarlane-Chard, 33 Percy Street,
London W1T 2DF. No performance may be given unless
a licence has been obtained.

No rights in incidental music or songs contained in the work
are hereby granted and performance rights for any
performance/presentation whatsoever must be obtained
from the respective copyright owners..

This book is sold subject to the condition that it shall not, by way
of trade or otherwise, be lent, resold, hired out, or otherwise circulated
in any form of binding or cover other than that in which it is published
and without a similar condition being imposed on the subsequent purchaser

For Eoin

The Abbey Theatre

Enlightenment

By Shelagh Stephenson

The Abbey Theatre gratefully acknowledges the financial
support from the Arts Council/An Chomhairle Ealaíon

the arts
council
schomhairle
ealaíon

Enlightenment

By Shelagh Stephenson

Enlightenment by Shelagh Stephenson was first performed at the Abbey Theatre, Dublin on 3 March 2005. Press night was 9 March 2005.

There will be one interval of 15 minutes

Cast in order of appearance

Lia	**Ingrid Craigie**
Nick	**Mark Lambert**
Mrs Tindle	**Jan Carey**
Gordon	**Alan Barry**
Joanna	**Amy Marston**
Adam	**Christopher Adlington**

Director	**Ben Barnes**
Designer	**Joe Vanek**
Lighting Designer	**Rupert Murray**
Sound	**Cormac Carroll**
Voice Director	**Andrea Ainsworth**
Stage Director	**John Stapleton**
Assistant Stage Manager	**Pamela McQueen**
Set	**Abbey Theatre Workshop**
Costumes	**Abbey Theatre Wardrobe Department**

Director of the Peacock	**Ali Curran**

Please note that the text of the play which appears in this volume may be changed during the rehearsal process and appear in a slightly altered form in performance.

Shelagh Stephenson *Author*

Shelagh has written several original radio plays, the most recent being the award-winning **Five Kinds of Silence** which she adapted for the stage, and which played at Hammersmith Lyric in 2000. Her first stage play, **The Memory of Water**, premiered at Hampstead Theatre, and subsequently transferred to the West End. In February 2000, it won an Olivier Award for Best Comedy. Her next play **An Experiment with an Air-Pump**, opened at the Royal Exchange Theatre in Manchester. It was joint recipient of the Peggy Ramsay Award, and later transferred to Hampstead Theatre. Both plays subsequently ran at New York's Manhattan Theatre Club, and **The Memory of Water** continues to be popular in productions all over the world. Her screen adaptation of the play, **Before You Go**, was released in 2002 starring Julie Walters. Other plays include **Ancient Lights**, which was produced at Hampstead Theatre in December 2000 and **Mappa Mundi**, produced in the Cottesloe at the Royal National Theatre in October 2002. In 2004 she won the prestigious Sloan Commission award in the United States and is currently completing a play for Manhattan Theatre Club.

Ben Barnes *Director*

Ben Barnes is Artistic Director of the Abbey Theatre and has recently overseen an extensive national and international programme to celebrate **abbey**onehundred, the centenary year of the Abbey Theatre. Among the highlights of the year were The Abbey and Europe season which featured visiting companies from across the continent and The Abbey and Ireland season which celebrated the richness and diversity of the Abbey repertoire with eighteen productions and readings to coincide with the 2004 Dublin Theatre Festival. The work of the Abbey during Mr Barnes' tenure has been extensively honoured at The Irish Times/ESB Awards, the Olivier Awards in London and the Tony Awards in New York. Highlights include the Tom Murphy retrospective of 2001, the European tour of **Translations**, twenty-five new works premiered on both stages, **Medea** with Fiona Shaw, **Barbaric Comedies** in Edinburgh and Dublin and **Hinterland** in Dublin and London. In 2004 he directed the centenary production of **The Playboy of the Western World** in Ireland and on tour throughout the United States, **The Gigli Concert** by Tom Murphy which opened the Energex Brisbane Festival and went on to play in Sydney and **Translations** by Brian Friel for Soulpepper in Toronto. He has directed close on fifty productions at the Abbey and his stage work has been seen in most major cities throughout the world. His production of **The Plough and the Stars** opened the Barbican international season in January of this year in London where it was a major critical and public success.

Joe Vanek *Designer*

Joe Vanek's designs for major Abbey shows since 1990 include **Dancing at Lughnasa, Wonderful Tennessee, Observe the Sons of Ulster Marching Towards the Somme, Angels in America, Macbeth, The Secret Fall of Constance Wilde, St. Joan, Love in the Title, Dolly West's Kitchen, Aristocrats** and **The Cherry Orchard**. Other recent designs include **Therese Raquin, b.a.s.h, The Shape of Things, Gates of Gold,** Brian Friel's **Performances** and **The Price** (Gate Theatre), David Hare's **Skylight** and David Mamet's **Boston Marriage** (Project), **Lady Macbeth of Mtsensk, The Silver Tassie** and **The Queen of Spades** (Opera Ireland). Work abroad includes **By The Bog of Cats** with Holly Hunter (USA), **Who's Afraid of Virginia Woolf?** (Denmark) and the opera, **The Makropulous Case** (Holland). He has just co-curated the **abbey**onehundred: Scene Change Exhibition at the Irish Museum of Modern Art (IMMA) and for CoisCéim Dance Theatre he designed David Bolger's **Nutcracker**. Future plans include Tom Mac Intyre's **What Happened Bridgie Cleary** at the Peacock and the Irish premiere of Edward Albee's **The Goat** for Landmark Productions at the Project.

Rupert Murray *Lighting Designer*

Rupert Murray is a freelance lighting designer and producer. As a lighting designer he has over one hundred and fifty credits around the world to his name. Recent designs for the Abbey and Peacock Theatres include Arthur Miller's **All My Sons,** Sean O'Casey's **The Plough and the Stars,** Aidan Mathews' **Communion,** Tom Murphy's **The Gigli Concert,** Brian Friel's **Aristocrats** and Dion Bouicault's **The Shaughraun**. For the Gate Theatre he designed Samuel Beckett's **Waiting for Godot,** Tennessee Williams' **The Eccentricities of a Nightingale,** Mark O'Rowe's **Crestfall,** Brian Friel's **Dancing at Lughnasa** and Bernard Farrell's **Many Happy Returns**. He designed Berthold Brecht's **The Life of Galileo** for Rough Magic Theatre Company, Tom Murphy's adaptation of **The Drunkard** for b*spoke theatre company and David Hare's **Skylight** for Landmark productions. He is the lighting designer for the international hit, **Riverdance - The Show**. Rupert was Festival Director of the St. Patrick's Festival from 1995 to 2000 and was a key member of the team that transformed Ireland's national celebrations. He has also been responsible for staging and directing the opening and closing festivities at the Wexford Festival Opera for the last five years and was Creative Director of the Opening Ceremony for the Special Olympics World Summer Games staged in Croke Park in June 2003.

Cormac Carroll *Sound Designer*

Cormac is from Sligo. Companies worked for in Ireland include Bloc One Theatre, The Hawks Well Theatre and the Gaiety. As Sound Designer at the Abbey his work includes **Observe the Sons of Ulster Marching Towards the Somme, I Do Not Like Thee Doctor Fell, Heavenly Bodies, Defender of the Faith, Finders Keepers, Aristocrats, She Stoops to Conquer, The House of Bernarda Alba, All My Sons, The Plough and the Stars, Ariel, Da, Eden, Communion,The Guys, For the Pleasure of Seeing Her Again, The Memory of Water, The Sanctuary Lamp, Made in China** and **The Morning After Optimism**. His work for Rough Magic includes **Shiver, Olga, Words of Advice for Young People** and **Take me Away**.

Christopher Adlington *Adam*

Christopher trained at the Royal Scottish Academy of Music and Drama. His theatre credits include **Poulet Philips** (Soho Theatre), **Bloody Poetry** (Brockley Jack Theatre), **Troilus and Cressida, Three Lives of Lucie Cabrol** (RSAMD), **Blue Remembered Hills, Hamlet** (Rep Theatre Company), **The Real Thing, Taste of Honey** (Manchester University), **Romeo and Juliet** (6 X 9 Theatre). Film and television credits include **Down to Earth** (BBC), **Elgar's Enigma** (BBC), **Take Three Girls** (Inspired Movies), **The Teacher** (New Alchemy Productions), **Raindogs** and **Red Rose** (Palm Tree UK). This is Christopher's first appearance at the Abbey Theatre.

Alan Barry *Gordon*

Alan Barry was born in Dublin and began his professional career with Anew MacMaster's Shakespeare Company. His London West-End appearances include **Whose Life Is It Anyway?** (Savoy), **Comedians** (Old Vic) and the musical **High Society** (Victoria Palace). Credits in Ireland include **Educating Rita** (Edwards-MacLiammóir Productions), Mr. Drumm in **Da** and **Run For Your Wife** (Olympia Theatre and tour), **Summer House** (Druid), **Triptych, You Can't Take It With You, Moonshine, Prayers of Sherkin, Chamber Music, The Duty Master** and **The Crucible** (Abbey Theatre), **Arrah-na-Pogue, The Recruiting Officer, Blithe Spirit, You Never Can Tell, The School for Scandal, Aristocrats, A Midsummer Night's Dream, London Assurance, A Tale of Two Cities, An Ideal Husband, A Streetcar Named Desire** and **Jane Eyre** (Gate Theatre). Film credits include **Evelyn, Robin Hood, A Love Divided, The General, Sweeney Todd, Some Mother's Son, In the Name of the Father, The Dirty Dozen** (The Next Mission), **Hennessy, Captain Nemo and The Floating City** and **Secret Places**. Television credits include **The Return** (Granada), **Fair City** (RTE), **Baddiel's Syndrome,** (Avalon/Sky), **Making the Cut** (RTE), **Ballykissangel** (BBC), **The Governor** (BBC) and **The Old Curiosity Shop** (Disney Channel).

Jan Carey *Mrs Tindle*

Jan trained at the Guildhall School of Music and Drama. New plays and English premieres include Bill Naughton's **Spring and Port Wine** (Birmingham Alex, Mermaid and Apollo Theatres, London), Vaclav Havel's **The Increased Difficulty in Concentration** and Rod Beacham's **No Big Deal** (Richmond Orange Tree), Vanessa Brook's **Let's Pretend** (Scarborough), Samuel Adamson's translation of Ibsen's **A Doll's House** (Southwark Playhouse) and Michael Frayn's translation of **The Seagull**, with a cast including Ingrid Craigie and directed by Patrick Mason. Other classics include **Man of Mode, Love's Labour's Lost** and **The Cherry Orchard** (Prospect Theatre Company), **Pygmalion** (Albery Theatre) and **The Importance of Being Earnest** (Glasgow Citizens). She has also played seasons at the Birmingham Rep, the Sheffield Crucible, Scarborough and Colchester. Television credits include **Smiley's People, Reith, Dr Finlay, Taggart, Memonto Mori, Two Thousand Acres of Skye, Pollyanna, I Claudius, Every Time You Look At Me, Bomber, Holby City** and **New Tricks**. Films include **A Man for All Seasons**. Jan has written and performed in a celebration of the life of the First World War poet/composer **Ivor Gurney: Author, Composer, Soldier of A Sort** which has played at festivals and twice sold out in the Purcell Room on London's South Bank. This is Jan's first appearance at the Abbey Theatre.

Ingrid Craigie *Lia*

Ingrid read English at Trinity College Dublin before joining the Abbey Theatre Company for five years where many appearances included **Our Town, Talbot's Box** (also at the Royal Court), **Mrs Warren's Profession, The Glass Menagerie, Aristocrats** and **A Life** (also at the Old Vic). Recent work at the Abbey and Peacock Theatres includes **Aristocrats, Ariel, Love in the Title** (also San Jose and Singapore), **The Map Maker's Sorrow, Wonderful Tennessee** (also on Broadway), **The Wexford Trilogy** (also at the Bush Theatre) and **The Plough and the Stars**. Other recent theatre includes **Boston Marriage, Copenhagen** (Project), **Stolen Child** (Andrew's Lane), **The Misanthrope, The Collection** (Gate Theatre), **The Cavalcaders** (Tricycle Theatre), **Crave** (Royal Court, Edinburgh Festival and European tour), **The Weir** (Centaur Theatre, Montreal), **Play** and **Come and Go** (Gate Theatre Beckett Festival at the Barbican), **Prayers of Sherkin** (Old Vic) and **The Colleen Bawn** (Royal Exchange Theatre, Manchester). Television and film credits include **Pure Mule, DDU, Ballykissangel, The Wexford Trilogy, Thou Shalt Not Kill, The Ballroom of Romance, The Dead, Da, The Railway Station Man, Widows Peak, A Man of No Importance, Circle of Friends, Spaghetti Slow** and **Benedict Arnold**.

Mark Lambert *Nick*

Mark's numerous productions at the Abbey include the premieres of **Observe the Sons of Ulster Marching Towards the Somme, Ariel** and **Barbaric Comedies,** for which he received an Irish Times/ESB Award nomination for Best Actor and **The Gigli Concert** which recently toured to Australia. Other fulfilling moments in his career include the premiere of **Our Country's Good** with the Royal Court, the premieres of Friel's **Molly Sweeney, A Month in the Country** and **Three Sisters** at the Gate Theatre and the Royal Court, **The Memory of Water** in the West End, **Juno and the Paycock** in the West End for which he was nominated for an Olivier Award and recently, **All's Well That Ends Well** with the RSC. Television and film credits include **Cracker, Frost, Dalziel and Pascoe, Bottom, The Young Ones, Veronica Guerin, Sharpe's Rifles, No Tears, Rosemary and Thyme, Evelyn, Borstal Boy, Durango, Proof** and **Vanity Fair**. Last year he directed **Baldi** a six part BBC radio series. He was an Associate Director of the Abbey where he has directed a number of productions.

Amy Marston *Joanna*

Amy's theatre work includes **After Mrs Rochester** (Shared Experience), **Snake in Fridge, Ghost Train Tattoo/Snapshots, Unidentified Human Remains** and **The True Nature of Love** (all at Manchester Royal Exchange), **Sitting Pretty** (Chelsea Theatre), **Eurydice** (Whitehall - West-End), **Gulliver's Travels** (Theatre Clwyd), **Yerma** (Bristol Old Vic) and **The Children's Hour** (National Theatre). Television credits include **Jericho, Quest III, He Knew He Was Right, Judge John Deed, Doctors, Plain Jane, Mrs Bradley's Mysteries, Where The Heart Is, Faith in the Future, Tom Jones, The Black Velvet Band, The Hello Girls, Neverwhere, Over Here, Bottom, 2.4 Children** and **Between the Lines**. Film includes **Charlotte Gray**. Amy is delighted to be making her debut at the Abbey Theatre.

Our warmest thanks go to

Sponsors

Anglo Irish Bank

CityJet

Ferndale Films

RTÉ

The Gulbenkian
Foundation

The Irish Times

The Sunday Tribune

Benefactors

Allied Irish Bank

Bank of Ireland

Behaviour & Attitudes
Marketing Research

Electricity Supply Board

Independent News &
Media Plc

Irish Life and
Permanent Plc

Merc Partners

Pfizer International
Bank Europe

SIPTU

Uni Credito Italiano
Bank (Ireland) Plc

Platinum Patrons

Terry Calvani & Sarah
Hill

Lillian & Robert
Chambers

Brian Halford

Donald Helme

Avine Lydon

Lorcan Lynch

Mercer Human
Resource Consulting

Lorna Mooney

Andrew & Delyth Parkes

Jean Saunders

Alan Sheil

Bill Shipsey

Adrian Timmons

Total Print & Design

Francis Wintle

Writer-in-Association

Sponsored by
Anglo Irish Bank

Hilary Fannin

Mark O'Rowe

Silver Patrons

Ron Rutler

Joe Byrne

Zita Byrne

Orla Cleary

Claire Cronin

Maretti D'Arcy

Pauline Fitzpatrick

Monica Flood

Paul & Florence Flynn

Prof. Nicholas Grene

Francis Keenan

Peter Kennan

Gerald Kelly & Co.
Builders Providers

Ciaran Nicholson &
David Lass

Mary T. Malone

Padraig Cartan

Mc Cullough – Mulvin
Architects

Frank & Evelyn Murray

Vincent O'Doherty

John P.H & Rosemary
O'Reilly

Sumitomo Mitsui
Finance Dublin

Margaret Tallon

Michael Stein

Abbey Theatre

Abbey Theatre Staff

BOARD

Eithne Healy *Chairman*

Loretta Brennan Glucksman

Eugene Downes

Niall O'Brien

John O'Mahony

Michael J. Somers

John Stapleton

Artistic Director
Ben Barnes

Managing Director
Brian Jackson

Executive Office
Orla Mulligan

abbeyonehundred
Anne Marie Kane
Sharon Murphy
Jennie Scanlon

Abbey Players
Clive Geraghty
Des Cave

Archive
Mairead Delaney

Assistant Stage Managers
Marella Boschi
Stephen Dempsey
Pamela McQueen

Box Office
Des Byrne
Clare Downey
Adam Lawlor

Box Office Clerks
Catherine Casey
Anne Marie Doyle
Lorraine Hanna
Iain Mullins
Maureen Robertson
David Windrim

Carpenters
Brian Comiskey
Kenneth Crowe
Mark Joseph Darley
John Kavanagh
Jonathon McDonnell
Kealan Murphy
Bart O'Farrell

Casting
Marie Kelly

Cleaning
Joe McNamara

Design
Laura Howe
Maree Kearns
Eimear Murphy

Development
Tina Connell
Aine Kiernan

Director of the Peacock
Ali Curran

Finance
Margaret Bradley
Margaret Flynn
Pat O'Connell

Front of House
Pauline Morrison
John Baynes

Hair and Make-Up
Patsy Giles

H.R. Manager
Ciaran McCallion

Honorary Associate Directors
Vincent Dowling
Tomás MacAnna

Information Technology
Dave O'Brien
Ivan Kavanagh

Lighting
Mick Doyle
Brian Fairbrother
Barry Madden
Kevin McFadden

Literary
Jocelyn Clarke
Orla Flanagan

Maintenance
Michael Loughnane

Outreach/Education
Elena Gamble
Michelle Howe
Jean O'Dwyer
Anne O'Gorman

Press & Marketing
Lynn Dormer
Lucy McKeever
Janice McAdam

Props
Stephen Molloy

Reception
Sandra Williams

Scenic Artists
Angie Benner
Rhonwen Hayes
Brian Hegarty
Jennifer Moonan

Sound
Richard Barragry
Eddie Breslin
Cormac Carroll

Stage Directors
Finola Eustace
Audrey Hession
John Stapleton

Stage Door
Patrick Gannon
Patrick Whelan

Stage Hands
Aaron Clear
Pat Dillon
Mick Doyle
Des Hegarty
Paul Kelly

Stage Managers
John Andrews
Gerry Doyle

Technical
Vanessa Fitz-Simon
Peter Rose
Tony Wakefield

Ushers
Stephen Brennan
Sarah Buckley
David Clarke
Con Doyle
John Durcan
Marie Claire Hoysted
Stephen Logne
Donna Murphy
Cillian O'Brien
Joseph O'Neill
Laura Pyne
Jim O'Keefe

Voice Director
Andrea Ainsworth

Wardrobe
Sandra Gibney
Marian Kelly
Vicky Miller
Sinead Lawlor
Niamh Lunny
Joan O'Clery

Advisory Council
Minister for Arts, Sport and Tourism
Minister for Finance
Kathleen Barrington
Frank Cuneen
Paddy Duffy
Clare Duignan
John Fairleigh
Clive Geraghty
Des Geraghty
Peadar Lamb
Fergus Linehan
John Lynch
Tomás MacAnna
Patricia McBride
Muriel McCarthy
Jimmy Murphy
Donal Nevin
Edna O'Brien
Ulick O'Connor
Pat O'Reilly
Peter Rose
John Stapleton

Enlightenment

Characters

Lia
Nick
Joyce
Gordon
Joanna
Adam

A Note on the Set

Naturalistic verisimilitude is not required. The lines of the room should be clean and stark, any details shown by projections, and changes of place and time achieved by lighting rather than naturalistic clutter.
The effect should be a cross between a Bill Viola video installation and a Dutch interior. At the beginning there are books and papers, a couple of items of furniture. By the end, the room is an empty box, lit like light inside an eggshell.

Act One

Scene One

Quietly hypnotic, trance-like music. A black stage.

In ultraviolet light, two tennis balls bounce across the stage. They are fired simultaneously from a wooden contraption. At first they bounce in tandem, hitting the ground at exactly the same time. Soon they're almost imperceptibly out of sync. By the time the balls have reached the other side of the stage, they're not in sync at all.

Lights up on **Lia**, *thirty-nine, her husband* **Nick**, *early forties. The corner of a room. One tall window, open. The rest of the set is suggested by back projections: books and paintings from floor to ceiling. A desk, laptop, papers, opened books.*

Lia *fires the balls again from the contraption and the same sequence occurs as they both watch.*

Lia   I wish I could remember what it was for.

Nick   Something to do with patterns.

Lia   Probability?

Nick   Minute fluctuations that you can't see.

Lia   So they bounce in unison . . . and gradually go out of sync.

Nick   He was trying to prove a thesis.

Lia   What exactly?

Nick   I can't remember.

Lia   Things fall apart?

Nick   Maybe.

Lia   I can't remember either.

She sets the contraption down and fires it again. They both watch.

It's like a letter we don't know how to translate.

Joyce Tindle *comes in. Late middle age, plain, neatly dressed.*

Joyce   What a lovely bathroom.

She sits down on a hard chair.

Lia   Thank you.

Joyce   D'you have anything that belongs to him?

Lia   Nick? Could you?

Nick   Like what?

Joyce   Anything. It doesn't matter.

Nick *goes out, with bad grace.*

Lia   I'm sorry. He's nervous.

Joyce   He's a man.

Lia   Yes.

Joyce   They're always less receptive. I wonder if I could have a glass of water?

Lia   Yes, of course.

She goes out. **Joyce** *gets up and takes in the room. Glances at the papers on the desk. Looks at the books on the shelves, the paintings. Sits down again as* **Lia** *returns with a glass of water.*

Joyce   You've got some lovely art.

Lia   Oh. Thank you.

Joyce   Paintings are like people in a room, aren't they?

Lia   I suppose they are, yes.

Nick *comes back carrying a guitar, a T-shirt and a sock.*

Nick   These are all his.

Joyce *takes the guitar.*

Joyce   Is he musical?

Nick   Not really.

Lia All young boys have guitars.

Joyce *strums a few out-of-tune cords, hands the guitar back and takes the sock.*

Joyce Has it been washed?

Nick I don't think so. It was under his bed.

Joyce *cradles the sock, rubs it. Silently. She takes the T-shirt, which has 'Coldplay' on the front, and holds it up. She folds it in her lap, stroking it.*

Nick Look, if you don't mind –

Lia Nick –

Joyce Whilst I remember. I know you're Lia and I know you're Nick. But I don't want to know anything else. I don't need to know your surnames. Is that all right?

Lia Of course.

Joyce It gets in the way.

Nick Of what?

She turns the sock and the T-shirt over and over.

Joyce You don't have to stay if you don't want, Nick. Some people find it disturbing. I understand that.

Lia I'd like you to stay.

Nick OK. OK.

He sits down at the swivel desk-chair, and folds his arms. **Joyce** *fans herself.*

Joyce Goodness, it's hot. What temperature d'you think it is?

Lia I think they said thirty degrees.

Joyce Which would be what?

Lia I'm sorry?

Joyce   In Fahrenheit.

Lia   I'm not sure. Very hot.

Nick   Eighty-five.

Joyce   I'm getting stone. Damp. I'm getting a rocky place. Quite sharp. And water.

Lia   Is there sea there?

Joyce   I'm not getting sea, no.

She looks at **Nick**.

Joyce   He's not your son, is he?

Nick   Not biologically, no.

Joyce   But you brought him up. You love him very much.

Nick   Forgive me, but you don't need to be psychic –

Joyce   I'm not a psychic dear, that's your word. I'm a sensitive. Ah. I know what it is. It's a cave.

Lia   He's in a cave?

Joyce   Possibly.

Expectant silence.

Nick   Well is he or isn't he?

Joyce   I'm not sure he's there now.

Lia   Has someone taken him there?

Joyce   There's water running down the walls. And I'm getting a sense of other people. I'm getting other voices.

Lia   What language are they speaking?

Joyce   It's not English. Could it be Arabic? Perhaps further east. I'm not a linguist but I get the sense it's not European. Oh. He does have lovely red hair, doesn't he? A very deep red. You could never call it ginger. Who does he get it from?

Lia   His father.

Joyce   Oh. Now this is most peculiar.

Lia   What?

Joyce   I'm getting crossed wires. I'm getting the letter F. I don't think it's got anything to do with Adam. Is there a Fiona?

Nick   No.

Joyce   It's a woman. And she passed over a very long time ago. Could it be Fanny?

Lia   Frances. Is it Frances?

Joyce   Frances! That's who it is. I've no idea what she wants but she's here.

Lia   Frances Hewer. Could it be her?

Joyce   Frances Hewer. Yes.

Lia   I've been reading her letters. I'm researching the Indian Mutiny. Her son was —

Joyce   She says everything's lovely.

Lia   She died about 1870.

Nick   Can we get back to Adam, d'you think?

Joyce   I'm just a vessel dear, I'm not in charge. (*She cocks her head to one side.*) She's gone now, you've obviously upset her.

Lia   D'you get the sense . . . Is Adam . . . is he alive?

Joyce   I get a very strong sense of him. He has such a lovely, open face, hasn't he? And I'm still getting the cave, but I'm fairly certain now he's not in it any more.

Lia   D'you sense anything else? Like fear?

Joyce   No. He's not afraid.

Lia   Is he alive?

Joyce   He's not speaking to me at all. I just get a sense of him.

Nick   A sense of him being what?

Pause.

Joyce   Unafraid.

Lia   You must know if he's alive or not.

Joyce   He has a very strong presence. I can't explain it any more than that. A very positive strength. Which could be described as a life force.

Lia   D'you have any feeling about where the cave might be?

Joyce   He's not there any more, dear.

Lia   No, I know, but –

Joyce   It's a funny thing, but I'm getting a big bowl of noodles. Not pasta. Noodles. Did he like noodles?

Nick   Not particularly.

Joyce   Well, that's what I'm getting. It could have nothing to do with him. It could be this Frances woman who had a taste for them. It's quite difficult. She keeps cutting in. Here she is again. You said something about her son?

Lia   Yes.

Joyce   She says she's found him. Does that mean anything to you?

Lia   He was killed at Lucknow in 1857.

Joyce   Ah yes. I'm getting spices. That would account for it.

Lia   They never found his body.

Joyce   She says they sliced him into ribbons. But now he's whole again. Oh. He's back.

Lia   Who?

Joyce   Your son. He's very handsome and he's been surfing. I can smell the salt spray in his hair. He's saying something. I can't make out what it is.

Silence. **Joyce** *turns the sock over and over, and closes her eyes.*

Lia D'you know where he is?

Joyce I'm trying. I'm trying.

Silence. She shakes her head.

I'm sorry. He's far away. That's all I know.

Lia But is he dead?

Joyce You mustn't think of it like that –

Lia So, yes. You're saying yes.

Joyce Death's not what you think it is.

Nick Death is being dead and being dead is death. Period.

Joyce It's just passing over to the other side.

Lia And you think Adam's on the other side?

Joyce I get a very strong sense of him, so strong, so clear, it makes me feel he's alive.

Lia But you don't know that?

Joyce I don't know anything dear. I'm just a vessel. I told you. He loves you very much. Both of you. I can feel that from him. I think that's what he's trying to say to me. In a wordless way.

Nick What's he using? Sign language?

Joyce I'm trying to read the essence. The energy. It's very difficult, Nick, because you're being rather negative, and when there's negativity in the room, the signals get mixed up. And then people like Frances pop in and confuse the issue. She's very determined and she's wearing a lot of very heavy Victorian clothing. All black. She's in mourning. Her presence is very strong in this room but she's very glad you're putting her in your book, Lia. She says it's time someone did.

Lia I don't know that I am putting her in a book.

Joyce   She seems to feel you ought to.

Joyce *cocks her head again*

She's off again.

She takes a sip of water, fans herself.

My nephew, Philip, he's forty years of age. What d'you think he does for a living?

Lia   I don't know.

Joyce   He's a guinea pig.

Lia   He is?

Joyce   Tests medicines for drugs companies. He's never had a job in his life. They call him Pharmaceutical Phil.

Nick   And how is he?

Joyce   Side effects are just part of the job. Does Adam dabble?

Lia   Excuse me?

Joyce   In drugs?

Nick   He's twenty years old. Probably.

Joyce   I'm wondering why Phil came into my mind, you see. I'm trying to make the connection. But as you say. Most young boys these days. If they're not smoking they're snorting.

Lia   You think Adam's muddled up with drugs?

Joyce   I'm trying to interpret the information I'm getting. It can be quite cryptic. On the other hand, guinea pigs could be the clue. Is he trying to tell me he's in South America? Isn't that where guinea pigs come from?

Nick   I don't know.

Joyce   It's a very long-winded way of telling me. So perhaps not.

Silence.

Waterfalls. I'm getting an enormous waterfall. And the name Gabriel. Does he have a friend named Gabriel?

Lia   Not as far as I know.

Joyce *laughs.*

Joyce   Oh, I see. Gabriel, angel, waterfalls. Angel Falls. Venezuela. Is there a likelihood he may have gone there?

Nick   I thought you were supposed to be telling us.

Joyce   He's had contact with a Venezuelan person. Or thing. I'm getting that very strongly.

Lia   When we last heard from him he was on the opposite side of the world.

Joyce   Perhaps he met a Venezuelan. They're very nice people. Very friendly. I have a cousin in Caracas who teaches chemistry.

Silence.

No money.

Lia   Adam?

Joyce   Venezuela.

Pause.

There's just a lot of din now. You know when you can't tune in the radio properly? It's a bit like that. It means I'm tired, so I should stop now.

She puts the sock down.

Did that help at all?

Lia   Thank you.

Nick   You haven't told us if he's alive or dead.

Joyce   I can't tell you facts, dear, because I'm dealing with the immaterial world. I can only tell you what I sense. I'm sorry if it wasn't enough.

Lia No, you've been very helpful. Truly. Obviously we'd love to know something for certain – it's been five months now, and it doesn't get easier, it gets worse. We went to Jakarta, we went to Bali, we went to Australia, even though I hate flying, every time I get on a plane I think we're going to be blown up. People said they might have seen him, but it was always maybe, nothing definite, nothing we could get hold of. We put posters up in backpackers' hostels. We tried a private detective. We tried a water-diviner, some woman who reads runes. Nothing. The police couldn't help, nobody could help, but my bones ache for him, my head is full of him, and sometimes I think my heart will burst –

She crumples into tears.

Joyce Why don't you call me again in a week or so, and we can have another go? How would that be?

Lia Maybe, I don't know.

Nick I think she needs a rest now. Thanks for coming, Mrs Tindle.

Joyce Joyce.

Nick We'll let you know if we need you again.

Lia *sits down on the desk chair, drying her eyes.*

Lia I'm sorry.

Joyce Don't despair. He wouldn't want you to do that. Your grandfather's name was Patrick, wasn't it?

Lia Yes.

Joyce He's standing behind your right shoulder and he's telling you not to despair. And the headaches aren't migraine. They're stress.

Lia OK.

Joyce *gets up.*

Joyce Anyway, dear, call me if you feel the need.

Lia   Adam had this dazzling smile. Did you get that?

Joyce   Yes.

Lia   I'm not saying it because I'm his mother. He walked into a room and people were slayed by him. He was magnetic. Is.

Joyce   I sensed it. I sensed that charisma. It's been lovely talking to you. You call me next week, and we'll have another little go. Goodbye, dear. Don't get up.

She goes out. **Nick** *looks at* **Lia**.

Nick   Where the *fuck* did you find *her*?

Lia   Stop it, don't.

She starts taking books from piles on the floor and putting them into boxes.

It's better than nothing. It's something. I just want to hear his voice. Sometimes I think I'll die if I don't hear his voice again.

Nick   We're not going to hear him through her.

Lia   Princess Diana used to go to her.

Nick   That's not a recommendation.

Lia   Some things she said were true.

Nick   Anybody could have guessed that stuff.

Lia   She knew my grandfather's name. She knew –

Nick   You told her most of it yourself.

Lia   She knew I was getting headaches.

Nick   There's a box of Anadin on your desk. She picks stuff up, she gathers information, she'll have sussed us out before she got here.

Lia   She doesn't know our surname –

Nick   And you believe that, do you?

Lia   She said she felt he was alive –

The phone goes. **Lia** *grabs it.*

Lia   Hello? . . . Hello?

Silence.

Hello?

Nick   Who is it?

Lia   I don't know.

She hands the phone to him. He listens.

Nick   No one there.

He puts it down. They both look at the phone.

Maybe they'll call back.

Silence.

Did they hang up on you? Or was no one there to begin with?

Lia   There was no one there.

Nick   OK.

Lia   But there must have been someone somewhere. Trying to call us. Phones don't ring spontaneously.

Nick   So they'll call back.

Pause. She taps the last-call number on the phone, listens.

Lia   'We do not have the caller's number.'

Pause.

I don't know why I do this. Every time the phone rings. My heart leaping. I know it's not him. It never is.

Nick   You still hope.

Pause.

Lia   When'll it stop, d'you think?

Nick   Possibly never.

Lia   Can you die of it?

Nick   One way or another.

Lia   How long will it feel like this?

Nick   Until it stops feeling like this.

Lia   And then?

Nick   And then I don't know.

Lia   Closure. That stupid, unimaginative word. If anyone else says it to me I'll punch them.

Nick   They mean well.

Lia   They mean you've done the beginning, you've done the middle, now get to the end, we're exhausted.

Nick   They mean we can't live in limbo for ever.

Lia   But there is no ending. It's not a story. They talk about accepting and moving on. As if it's something you can recover from, like a broken ankle. What is it we're supposed to accept?

Nick   That he's not coming back.

Lia   You can't accept to order. Your heart has to catch up with your head and I don't know how to make that happen. Plus, I don't want to –

Nick   OK –

Lia   – because if I do, it's bad faith, it's giving up on him, and I have to stick with him, otherwise –

Nick   I know –

Lia   – it's disloyalty, it's betrayal –

Nick   I know –

Lia   You don't know! He's not your son.

Nick You wield this at me like a blunt instrument.

Lia It's true.

Nick It's irrelevant.

Lia It doesn't feel irrelevant.

Nick So stop feeling, and use your head.

Lia Don't tell me to be rational! Don't tell me what I should and shouldn't feel. We've done rational! Where did it get us?

Nick There are still practical things-

Lia Like what?

Nick The police haven't given up –

Lia The police were the ones who suggested a medium –

Nick The consulates, the embassies –

Lia They don't care.

Nick Lia –

Lia How am I supposed to get through another forty years of this? Last night I dreamt someone left his head in a bag outside a supermarket. I can't live like this. I'm frightened to go to sleep. I'm frightened to wake up.

Nick I don't think you should see any more psychics.

Lia She's not a psychic.

Nick Correct.

Lia She got noodles. He was in Indonesia –

Nick It's been in the papers, Lia.

Lia But she kept talking about a cave, which means he didn't – he wasn't caught in the bomb –

Nick She just says the first thing that comes into her head.

Lia But what if it's true about the cave?

Nick It's not. In your heart, you know it's not.

Lia If I could just see him one more time. If he would just give me a signal. I'm looking for him everywhere. Last week I dreamt I bumped into him in the tube and I said, where have you been? And he said, oh, I moved to Libya, didn't they tell you? And I said, can I have your phone number? And he said, no, there are no phone lines here. It's against the law.

Nick You told me this.

Lia I'm sorry. That's why people talk about moving on, isn't it? Because we've become crap company. There's only so much affliction they can bear.

Silence.

I just think that if he was in the Jakarta bombing they'd have found something. A shoe, something. Can a bomb just vaporise you?

Nick Probably.

Lia What would it feel like to vaporise?

Nick I'm not even going to think about it.

Lia At the very least he'd have felt terror.

Nick He wouldn't have known anything about it.

Lia Terror like we've never known.

Nick He probably wasn't even there.

Lia Because someone would have seen him in the vicinity. Beforehand. Wouldn't they?

Nick I would have thought so.

Lia If he's alive somewhere –

Nick He would have contacted us.

Lia But if he's in a cave –

Nick   He's not in a cave.

Lia   Somewhere without electricity. Without access to the outside world.

Nick   How?

Lia   Because someone's keeping him there.

Nick   Why?

Lia   That's what happens. Unspeakable things. Half the world's full of chaos and fury. They keep people in pits full of scorpions and then leave their heads on the side of the road. They cut their throats and send you the video. Worse things.

Nick   But we've always known these things. We knew these things before he went. Or if we didn't, it was wilful ignorance.

Lia   Before they were on the television. Now they've moved into our house.

Nick   I think you should go to the doctor. Get some tablets. To stop you imagining this stuff.

Lia   So I'll stop talking about it.

Nick   What good does it do?

Lia   You must imagine it, too.

Nick   As soon as I see severed limbs and crushed heads I wipe them out of my mind. I think about cookery. Football. Sex. Things I don't even care about, like golf. Anything. I mark essays. I go to the gym.

Lia   Things have to be faced.

Nick   They're chimeras, they're not real. Whatever happened to Adam is over. It lasted for seconds or minutes, and it ended.

Lia   We don't know that.

Nick   We keep coming back to this.

Lia We keep coming back to everything. It's hell.

Silence.

I'm so tired I could die.

Nick Why don't you go and lie down?

Lia Because I'll fall asleep and forget he's gone, and when I wake up I'll have to remember it all over again. Fresh minted. Like a sharp new penny.

Pause.

Nick I've some papers to mark. I should do them.

Lia If we didn't have work, if we were just sitting in the sand in a desert somewhere, and we'd lost our only child . . . Can you imagine? It's happening to someone right now as we speak. I'd never move again, I'd just sit there till the sun burned through my bones and I turned to dust.

Nick Why don't we both do a couple of hours, and then maybe go out?

Lia Some people just disappear. They leave their clothes on a beach and pretend they've drowned.

Nick Middle-aged men do that. Middle-aged men with bankruptcy orders and machete-wielding creditors.

Lia D'you think he's in Venezuela?

Nick No.

Lia Neither do I.

Pause.

It's odd, though. It's so specific.

Nick It's a technique, Lia.

Lia I wish I was drunk and I could stop thinking.

Nick Why don't you try and do some work?

Lia This woman whose son died at Lucknow. Frances
Hewer. She had three other children. She only lost one of
them. D'you think that made it easier?

Nick No.

Lia She went native. Did I tell you that? She went to
India to find his body and never came back. When she died
she was wearing a sari and living in a bare mud bungalow
with a cow.

Nick Was she happy?

Lia Something happened.

Nick What?

Lia I don't know, but it haunts me. She started out a
middle-class Victorian matriarch. And ended up in that bare
hut. No possessions, no status, no comfort. Facing the world
with nothing. Like a pure flame.

Nick I'll do those papers.

Lia Do I seem strange to you?

Nick Of course.

Lia You do too.

Nick We've become strange.

Lia As if there's a filter on the lens.

Nick Yes.

Lia You haven't kissed me for ages.

Nick I thought you didn't want me to.

He kisses her. She moves away.

Shall we go out later?

Lia Where?

Nick A film, maybe.

Lia   I'm just worried.

Nick   He won't call.

Lia   If it was a comedy, and we laughed –

Nick   That would be good.

Lia   I'll think about it.

Nick   You have laughed. You laughed at a James Thurber cartoon. About a cast-iron lawn dog.

Lia *smiles.*

Lia   I was drunk.

Pause.

D'you think I'm drinking too much?

Nick   That's not why I brought it up.

Lia   But am I?

Nick   Everyone drinks too much. Nobody has only one glass a night except in books. Or California.

Lia   But a whole bottle.

Nick   Is probably too much. Under normal circumstances.

Lia   Which these aren't.

Nick   No.

Lia   Will they ever be normal?

Nick   Probably not.

Lia   So I'll die an alcoholic.

Nick   No.

Lia   It's that or madness.

Pause.

Nick   D'you send him e-mails?

Pause.

Lia Why?

Nick I do.

Pause.

Lia I'm glad it's not just me.

Nick It's like writing a letter to Father Christmas and sending it up the chimney.

Lia Except Father Christmas doesn't exist.

Nick No.

Lia Every time it says 'You have e-mail', there's a tiny flutter inside me. Even when I'm convinced he's dead I still hope he might e-mail me. From Hades or somewhere.

Nick Anyway. I'd better do those papers.

Lia Yeah. You'd better.

He goes out. She picks up Adam's T-shirt and presses it against her face.

Scene Two

Next day. Same room: most of the paintings have gone. **Lia** *has a pile on the floor which she's wiping with a rag. She's dusty, dressed in the sort of clothes you wear for cleaning. Her father,* **Gordon,** *is introducing her to* **Joanna,** *thirty-ish. He's a retired Labour MP in his sixties.*

Gordon This is Joanna. My daughter, Lia.

Joanna Joanna Riley. It's great to meet you, Lia. Really great.

Lia Thank you.

Gordon Joanna's going to help us.

Lia I'm sorry?

Gordon Sit down, sit down –

He pulls out a chair for **Joanna**.

Lia How d'you mean, help us?

Joanna Obviously there's no guarantee,

Lia Who are you?

Gordon This is Joanna Riley. I told you.

Lia Told me what?

Joanna I'm so sorry. Did he not say? Did he not tell you?

Gordon I told you I was talking to her.

Joanna (*to* **Gordon**) I thought you'd had a conversation about this? I'm so sorry, Lia, I thought – Would you like me to go?

Lia No, of course not, please.

Joanna With your father's high profile, we thought there'd be a lot of interest –

Lia I'm sorry?

Joanna 'Former Labour Minister's grandson disappears.' People are bound to be interested. Which is good. We're on your side. All we want to do is help you tell your story.

Lia I'm sorry. Who are you?

Joanna I'm a documentary producer. We know how distressing the last few months must have been for you, and that's what we'd like to try and get across to people –

Lia Why?

Joanna Excuse me?

Lia It's already been in the papers. Nothing happened. No one came forward except two girls who met him in Sydney, and his friend Tom who last saw him when he said he was going to Jakarta.

Joanna   I've seen those articles, and they weren't very high profile. There was a lot of other news around at the time and they got a bit shunted. To somewhere halfway down page five.

Lia   There's still a lot of other news around. Hadn't you noticed? People are hacking each other to pieces. Blowing each other up. Lopping off limbs and disembowelling babies. Young men are exploding themselves all over the world.

Joanna   This would be television, Lia.

Lia   I wish you'd told me you were doing this.

Gordon   I'm only trying to help.

Joanna   Shall I just tell you a bit about the programme?

Lia   Would I have to be on it?

Joanna   I'm sorry?

Lia   The television.

Joanna   Would that be a problem?

Lia   I don't think I'd want to do that. I'm sorry.

Joanna   It's a serious piece, there'd be nothing sensationalist about it. We're looking at two cases of teenagers who've disappeared: a young girl called Miriam, and Adam. The aim is to find out what's happened. These things do jog people's memories. There'll be a number at the end that they can phone.

Lia   I'm sorry. I just feel as if this has been sprung on me out of nowhere.

Gordon   It's not out of bloody nowhere –

Joanna   I'm incredibly hot, I wonder if I could have a cold drink, Lia? Water would do.

Lia   Sorry, I'll get you some.

She makes to go, but **Joanna** *gets up.*

Joanna Please, just tell me where to go.

Lia The kitchen's down the corridor on the left. There are drinks in the fridge.

Joanna Thank you.

She goes out.

Lia Are you having an affair with her?

Gordon Why can't you take things at face value?

Lia Are you?

Gordon No.

She looks hard at him.

She's thirty-one years old.

Lia Yes? And?

Gordon And I'm not having an affair with her.

Pause.

Lia I'm sorry. I know you're trying to help. I don't want to do it, that's all.

Gordon We've got to do something.

Lia Not this.

Gordon Television's a very potent medium.

Lia I don't want to talk about how I feel. It's private.

Gordon You'd be talking about Adam.

Lia Adam's not a commodity.

Gordon It might jog someone's memory.

Lia It won't bring him back.

Gordon How do you know?

Joanna *comes back with a tray of beers.*

Joanna   I'm sorry, d'you mind? They looked so tempting.

She hands round three glasses of beer.

Just to take the edge off things. Cheers.

Lia   I was trying to get some work done.

Joanna   That must be so difficult for you at the moment, Lia.

Lia   Because you're sitting in my study.

Gordon   Now, now girls.

Joanna   I'm a mother myself, Lia. I can imagine what you must be going through.

Lia   You don't have to be a mother.

Joanna   I think only mothers can truly understand, don't you?

Lia   I have childless friends. It's not beyond their imagination.

Gordon   We're getting off on the wrong foot entirely here. Joanna is offering to help us. We're never going to find Adam unless we make a bit of a splash. At the moment nobody cares except us. There are wars out there, there are famines. What's one boy?

Joanna   There are so many voices out there, clamouring for attention, Lia, it's easy to get drowned out. But we can make your voice heard. You can say whatever you want to say. As much or as little as you like. I can't guarantee what might happen as a result, but I can guarantee it will do no harm. And it might do some good.

Gordon   What d'you think?

Lia   It doesn't feel right. I'm not that sort of person. I don't want my picture in the papers looking griefstricken.

Joanna   We wouldn't do that to you, Lia. You could look any way you wanted.

Gordon It's not about you, it's about Adam.

Lia All right. All right.

Joanna Is that a yes?

Lia No. It's an 'I don't know'. I'll think about it.

Joanna I'd have thought any mother in your position would be very keen to get her story across.

Lia I don't have a story. My son went off round the world and never came back. That's it.

Joanna You know it isn't.

Lia So you tell me what it is. You tell me.

Gordon Why are you behaving as if we're against you?

Joanna I know, it's very painful –

Lia Please don't use that word.

Joanna What?

Lia That normalising cliché. What's happening to us isn't painful. It's untenable, it's eating our hearts away. It's like having the whole of your life wiped out and only this one thing remains: he's disappeared and he's not coming back *and we're never going to find out what happened.*

Joanna I'm so sorry.

Pause.

Look, what I'm going to do is this.

She gets up, and rummages in her bag.

I'm going to leave you my card, and you can think about it. Call me at any time, day or night. Or e-mail me. Whatever. I'd love to hear from you, you know that, but I won't press my suit any further. And I'm going to go now, and leave you to mull it over with your father. It's been an honour, Lia, thanks for giving up your time. Gordon, we'll speak.

She goes.

Lia What does she mean, 'It's been an honour'?

Gordon She has an unfortunate manner. It's not her fault.
It's the world she moves in.

Lia I hate her.

Gordon Right.

Pause.

That's not a good start.

Lia How many times did she say my name? 'Oh, *Lia*,
I know exactly how you feel.' I hate her.

Gordon We've established that.

Lia How could you bring her here?

Gordon I think you're reacting irrationally.

Lia You are having an affair with her, aren't you?

Gordon No.

Pause.

I've taken her to dinner a couple of times.

Lia Right. The fog's lifting.

Gordon She's actually a very decent woman.

Lia How did you meet her?

Gordon She phoned me up. She'd read about it. I said
I thought the programme was a good idea.

Lia But you didn't think to ask me?

Gordon Well, he's my bloody grandson, he's not just your
son. You don't own him.

Lia OK. You do it. You do the documentary. You're the
one who likes being on television.

Gordon   What does that mean?

Lia   Even in *Today in Parliament* you were always shuffling your bottom along the bench so you'll be in shot.

Gordon   Was I bollocks.

Lia   I'd rather not do it, that's all.

Gordon   All right. All right.

Pause.

Lia   It's his twenty-first birthday next week.

Gordon   I know.

Silence.

Lia   You didn't want me to have him.

Gordon   Pregnant student with no sign of boyfriend. D'you blame me?

Lia   You said it would ruin my life.

Gordon   I was wrong. I'm sorry. What can I say?

Pause.

Lia   Is it our fault, d'you think?

Gordon   What?

Lia   Did we do something wrong?

Gordon   You can't blame yourself.

Lia   Not me. All of us.

Gordon   Meaning what?

Lia   As if the world's tilted so that all the money and all the power slips one way. To people like us.

Gordon   You don't have any power in a situation like this.

Lia   Exactly.

Gordon   Exactly what?

Lia   Now we feel powerless and that's what they want. They want us to know what it feels like.

Gordon   Who?

Lia   The people who did it.

Gordon   What are we talking about here?

Lia   Somebody has done something terrible to him.

Gordon   No. We don't know that.

Lia   He's out there and he's been swallowed up by something and it's not personal.

Gordon   What d'you think has swallowed him up?

Lia   You first.

Gordon   I'm not sure he has been.

Lia   So tell me what you do think. In your blackest moments. At three in the morning when you can't sleep.

Pause.

Gordon   That he's dead. I think that he's dead.

Lia   And what d'you imagine might have happened to him?

Gordon   He drowned. He fell down a ravine. He was run over and he had no papers on him.

Lia   You're lying.

Gordon   I'm not.

Lia   Those aren't your blackest thoughts. Those are the best worst case scenarios. We can't talk about the other ones. They're unsayable.

Gordon   If he'd been kidnapped they'd have made demands. That's the point of kidnapping.

Lia   At three o'clock in the morning, this is what I think. I think somebody killed him. They killed him – God, I don't know how I'm uttering the words, I have to detach myself from what I'm actually saying – they killed him because he's white and western and they hated him. And it wasn't personal. Which somehow makes it worse.

Gordon That's your nightmare. It doesn't mean it's true.

Lia And I wonder, at what point did he know? At what point did he lose hope? That's what keeps me awake. That's what makes my heart drop like a stone.

Pause.

Gordon The world's a very unstable place.

Lia And it's our fault.

Gordon If he's dead it's the fault of the people who did it.

Lia We screwed up. I sent him out into a world which we've completely fucked up, and somehow thought he'd be immune. That he'd be safe. How could he be?

Gordon Because thousands of kids go on holiday every day and ninety-nine point nine per cent come back.

Lia But it's not random that he didn't. It's not arbitrary. It looks like that, but it isn't.

Gordon Of course it's bloody random. It's not part of some greater scheme, there's no design in it. Adam never harmed a fly. Who'd want to harm him?

Lia A whole series of things, some big, some small, some imperceptible, some obvious, they all caused it to happen –

Gordon What? Caused what to happen?

Lia Whatever it was that happened. I misled him. I allowed him to believe that because he was a good, decent, person, he'd be blessed wherever he went. That because he cared about the state of the world, and he did, the world would care about him. I may even have half-believed it. I sent him to his death.

Gordon   Stop it. You don't know what happened to him. It could have been anything.

Lia   We're telling our children lies about what they deserve, about what they can take from the world as if it's their right.

Gordon   It's not your fault, Lia.

Lia   It is. Why d'you refuse to see it?

Gordon   You're overwrought, which is understandable, but you're wrong.

Silence.

Lia   I'm sorry. I'm on a wheel and I can't get off.

Gordon   That's why I think you should do this programme. It might help you to do just that.

Lia   Or I might find myself on another wheel entirely.

Gordon   Yes.

Lia   It would still be a wheel.

Nick *comes in.*

Nick   I've just been talking to Joanna.

Lia *(astonished)*   You know her?

Nick   No, I just met her.

Lia   She just left.

Nick   On her way out. I bumped into her. She seems great.

Lia   She's horrible.

Nick   Oh. Is she?

Gordon   No.

Lia   She is.

Gordon   There's been a misunderstanding. We all got off on the wrong foot.

Lia Only a mother can really understand. *Vomit.*

Nick Sorry?

Lia She said things like that.

Gordon There's obviously some female thing going on here that I'm not party to –

Nick She seemed perfectly nice to me.

Gordon She wants to help, that's all.

Nick I think she's all right, honestly. What's the problem?

Lia OK, I'm sorry. It's probably not her. It's just I don't want him captured on the television screen and diminished. I don't want him summed up. I don't want to see his face staring out at me from publicity shots, like one of those dead people. I don't want him to be lining the cat's litter box two days later. So tell her the answer is no, OK?

Blackout.

Scene Three

Lights up on same room. One week later.

*The room is completely bare apart from **Lia**'s desk and chair and two other hard chairs.*

Lia and **Nick** are with **Joanna** who has a tape recorder set up.

Joanna This is just kind of preliminary background stuff. Is that OK?

Lia Sure.

Joanna I've already talked to Gordon, who tells me Adam was a great surfer. Is that right?

Lia I don't know if he's great. He quite likes it.

Joanna You still talk about him in the present tense.

Lia Sometimes I do and sometimes I don't.

Joanna They use something called sex-wax, don't they?

Lia I'm sorry?

Joanna Surfers.

Nick It's resin. To stop their feet sliding off the board.

Joanna Is that all? How disappointing. Anyway. I'm so sorry. Let's get back to Adam. When did you last hear from him?

Lia In an e-mail. Five months ago. He said he was thinking of going to Jakarta.

Joanna And was it a very loving e-mail?

Lia Just normal.

Joanna But he was normally very loving?

Lia He was twenty years old. He was very independent.

Nick He didn't say, 'I love you, Mom,' all the time. He wasn't in an American movie.

Joanna Tell me a bit about him. What did he like doing?

Nick He was really interested in cold fusion.

Joanna Right.

Pause.

What is that exactly?

Nick The production of radioactive energy without heat. The general consensus is that it can't be done.

Joanna So he was a bit of a brain-box?

Lia No. He was quite clever.

Joanna What sort of hobbies did he have? It would be great if you had some photos of him, surfing or horse-riding, or playing football, whatever. Home videos, even better.

Lia Reading. He liked reading.

Joanna Anything a bit more dynamic?

Nick Like what?

Joanna Anything to get a sense of Adam the twenty-year-old boy who loved surfing and − I don't know, did he have a girlfriend, for example? Could we talk to her?

A beat.

Lia He's gay.

Joanna Right.

A beat.

And that wasn't . . . problematical in any way?

Lia For him or for us?

Joanna Either, I suppose.

Nick It wasn't for us. I hope it wasn't for him.

Lia It wasn't.

Joanna What I'm trying to do is get a picture. A warm, sympathetic picture that everybody can relate to.

Lia So you'd like us to miss out the gay bit?

Joanna Of course not, not at all. If he had a boyfriend maybe we could interview him?

Nick He didn't. Not that we know of.

Joanna Right. That's a pity.

Pause.

The thing is, most people don't really relate to cold fusion, do they? Or God, maybe they do and I'm out of touch. Am I?

Lia It's relatively esoteric.

Joanna   Yeah. I'm just thinking most people don't know what it is. And reading's a little bit on the bland side.

Nick   Your researcher asked us to dig out some photos. We'll get them to you as soon as we can.

Joanna   Great, great. Because television is essentially a visual medium. What about videos?

Lia   Those too. Can you make sure we get them back afterwards?

Joanna   We'll guard them with our life, don't worry.

Lia   They're all we have left.

Joanna   Of course. I understand. I'm going to try and build up a picture of Adam, so that people say, oh my God, that could be my son. So we get immediate identification. I might leave out the cold fusion and the reading because people don't respond to intellectuals, unfortunately; it's a sign of the times. And this isn't me speaking, incidentally, it's the people who pay my wages. But I think they'd really go for the surfing angle.

Lia   He didn't really do that much surfing.

Joanna   That's OK. The other people we're doing –

Lia   What other people?

Joanna   One's the young girl I told you about. Just got a place at RADA, a real star in the making, she disappeared in Cornwall. The other's a man who disappeared in the Australian Outback. A hang-glider. We've also got a standard guy-who-went-to-work-and-never-came-back. With a twist, because he was a cross-dresser.

Lia   I thought it was only about Adam and the girl?

Joanna   The network decided they want to broaden the focus.

Nick   You never mentioned this before.

Joanna I'm sure I did.

Lia You didn't.

Joanna Don't worry. Adam will be given a fair crack of the whip. And my feeling is that someone out there in the audience will recognise him, and they'll remember meeting him on their travels.

Nick So how long is this programme?

Joanna It's an ITV hour.

Lia What's that?

Joanna Four commercial breaks. Fifty-two minutes.

Nick That's about thirteen minutes each.

Joanna A bit less if you include titles and credits.

Lia It doesn't seem very much.

Joanna Television's very potent, you don't really need that long. Plus people have a very short attention span. And what we don't want them to do is channel surf.

Lia Right.

A beat.

Joanna Can I just ask you something?

Nick Go ahead.

Joanna What do you think has happened to Adam?

Lia He's been kidnapped by aliens for a breeding programme. That's the level I'm at.

Joanna Are you serious?

Lia What do you think?

Nick We don't know. We've been through every conceivable scenario and drawn a blank. We're in limbo. A door opened and we stepped out into thin air.

A beat.

Joanna   In your heart, d'you think he's alive?

Lia   I can't say. It's too complicated.

Nick   Can we leave it at that just now?

Joanna   Of course. I'm sorry.

She gets up and turns off the tape.

Maybe we'll pick this up some other time. You've both been great, thank you so much.

She looks at her watch and gathers up her stuff.

I've got a conference call, so I must dash. I'll call you tomorrow to arrange the shooting days, is that all right?

Lia   Yes, fine . . .

Joanna *looks round the room.*

Joanna   Not moving out, are you?

Lia   No.

Joanna   Spring cleaning?

Lia   I'm getting rid of stuff.

Joanna   Bit radical.

Lia   Yes.

Nick   Have you only just noticed?

Joanna   I didn't like to mention it. It could have been the bailiffs. Anything.

Lia   I'm trying to change things. My life.

Joanna   Ah.

Lia   What d'you mean, 'Ah'?

Joanna   Just, I understand.

Lia   Do you?

Joanna *looks round the room.*

Joanna   Actually, I'll come clean. I don't.

Lia   I can't put it into words.

Joanna   Right.

Pause.

Lia   I have too much stuff in my life.

Joanna   Oh, right. You're going for a more minimalist look?

Lia   No.

Nick   It's more complicated than that. Or more simple.

Joanna   Oooh. Mr Deep.

Lia   It doesn't have anything to do with interior decorating.

Joanna   Those books and paintings looked really lovely. They gave you a real idea of what sort of person you are. I wonder if you could put them back before the shoot? We need to have you in some sort of context.

Lia   I can't put them back. They're parcelled up to be given away.

Joanna   What?

Nick   Couldn't we shoot it somewhere else?

Joanna   Weren't they worth a lot of money?

Lia   Probably.

Joanna   But you're *giving them away?*

Lia   I don't want to talk about it, if that's OK.

Joanna   Who to?

Lia   Honestly, I'd rather not go into it.

Joanna   Why didn't you sell them if you didn't want them?

Lia   Can I just say I don't know?

Joanna   God. That is incredible.

Lia   Yes.

Joanna   You're mad.

Lia   Probably.

Joanna   Oh God, I'm sorry. You're not, I mean even if you were, it'd be understandable, I mean, look, I'm a mother –

Lia   Did you say you had a conference call?

Joanna   I'm sorry I said you were mad, I didn't mean it literally, I just –

Nick   It's OK. Like I said, it's complicated, and can we just leave it at that?

Joanna   Of course, of course. I'd better go, before I make a complete dick of myself, hadn't I?

She gathers up the rest of her stuff.

I'll call you tomorrow. OK?

She goes.

Lia   Thank you.

Nick   For what?

Lia   Being supportive. Pretending you understand why I got rid of everything.

Nick   I'm not pretending.

Lia   So what am I doing?

Nick   You're doing a Frances Hewer.

Lia   Am I?

Nick   Well, aren't you?

Lia   I feel as if I'm drowning in *stuff*.

Nick   Exactly.

Lia   As if my life has been dedicated to the accumulation of meaningless junk. In the hope that it might define me.

Nick   What you've just described is what everybody does.

Lia   I know. And I'd like to stop.

Nick   The Bermuda Triangle where materialism and capitalism meet the fatal concept of good taste. We're all sucked in.

Lia   I'm trying to pull myself out.

Nick   OK. You've divested yourself of all your trappings. D'you feel any better?

Lia   Not so far. No.

Blackout.

Scene Four

A park bench. One week later. It's very hot. **Lia** *is with* **Joyce Tindle**, *who is cradling Adam's T-shirt.*

Lia   When he was three years old, I was about to dismantle his cot because it was time for him to have a proper bed. And he came into the room, and climbed into his cot and said, I just want one last go before I have to grow up. He lay there, crooning like a baby, and I started to cry, because I realised he understood loss and yearning, and it seemed too early for him to know these things.

Silence.

He could cook. That's quite unusual for a young boy.

Silence.

And he had this way of running downstairs. Two at a time, but with no perceptible effort.

Silence.

Sometimes I phone him up.

Joyce   What number d'you dial?

Lia   I just pick up the phone and speak. I pretend he's on the other end. I pretend he's come back.

Joyce   D'you ever hear him?

Lia   All the time. In my head.

Joyce   He's trying very hard to get through.

Lia   Whilst I'm having these conversations with him, for two or three minutes I believe they're real. For two or three minutes it's as if he's alive. And I'm happy.

Pause.

Maybe that's what happiness is. Something you invent.

Joyce   I'm getting someone with a very odd name. Could it be Dingle?

Lia   My maternal grandfather.

Joyce   He's smiling.

Lia   Does he know anything about Adam?

Joyce   He says to tell you it was his father who went to Venezuela. Your great-grandfather.

Lia   It was nothing to do with Adam?

Joyce   That was my fault dear. I misunderstood. He's got a set of golf clubs.

Lia   Who has?

Joyce   Dingle.

Lia   Do they play golf in . . . on . . . the other side?

Joyce   Oh yes, dear. They do everything we do, but without the pain and the ego.

Lia   Is Adam with him?

Joyce   He says you mustn't worry.

Lia   Could you tell him that's not terribly helpful?

Joyce   I can't pass on messages I'm afraid. It's one-way traffic.

Silence.

He says life is a long quiet river.

Lia   What?

Joyce   Life is a long quiet river.

Lia   What does that mean?

Joyce   I've no idea. I'm just a conduit.

Lia   I think it's a French film.

Joyce   Is it, dear?

Lia   *La vie est une longue fleuve tranquille.*

Joyce   Oh, he's off.

Lia   There's a family in it called the Groseilles. The Gooseberries.

Joyce   They can be very cryptic. The spirit mind works in mysterious ways.

Pause.

I'm afraid it's gone quiet. But I'm sure someone else will be along in a minute.

Silence.

Lia   Nick doesn't like me seeing you.

Joyce   I know.

Pause.

Lia   I've decided I want to be a better person. I want to be good.

Joyce   That's admirable.

Lia   I mean consciously, thoughtfully, minutely good.

Joyce   I see.

Lia   I know what you're thinking, you're thinking it's some sort of penance because we lost our child.

Joyce   I don't judge.

Lia   It's not about Adam.

Joyce   Why d'you feel you need to be good?

Lia   Because the world is so very . . . cruel.

Joyce   There are more good people than bad people in the world. The bad have a disproportionate effect, that's all.

Lia   I don't believe that people are evil, do you?

Joyce   Oh yes. Some people are irredeemable.

Lia   I don't believe that.

Joyce   Even if they killed your son?

Lia   People are driven to things. They have grievances or illnesses. They're desperate.

Joyce   That really is just fluffy nonsense, dear. And I'm not sure I believe you.

Lia   I worry. Are we wealthy at someone else's expense?

Joyce   I'm not with you, dear.

Lia   We can only be rich because half the world's poor.

Joyce   I'm not au fait with the material and political world. You'd need to speak to an economist.

Lia   Nick says the figures don't add up.

Joyce   You can't solve the world's problems on your own.

Lia   I felt I ought to do something. I've packed all my stuff up to go to a charity auction. It seems completely pointless now. It's a drop in the ocean. It doesn't mean anything. My study's uncomfortable and depressing. I thought I'd get a sense of spiritual cleansing. I thought I'd get clarity of vision. Nothing's changed. I feel exactly the same.

Joyce   Perhaps it's not about how you feel.

Lia   Meaning?

Joyce   You give because it does good, not because it makes you feel better.

Lia   Nothing will ever make me feel better.

Joyce   I'm getting that Frances woman again. She's picked you the most enormous bunch of flowers. Can you smell them?

Lia *sniffs.*

Lia   No.

Joyce   Sweet peas. She says you worry too much and you drink too much coffee. She's concerned about you.

Lia   Ask her if she understands what I'm doing.

Joyce   She says of course she does but it doesn't detract from what she said about the coffee.

Lia   Is Adam with her?

Joyce   She says she hasn't seen him yet.

Lia   What does she mean, 'yet'?

Lia*'s mobile goes. She scrabbles around in her bag to find it.*

Lia   Hello? Oh, hi, Dad.

She listens in stunned silence.

Say that again.

She listens.

Oh my God.

She's in a state of shock.

Oh my God . . .

She listens

Where? . . . I don't understand . . . I just . . . Oh Jesus . . .
Yes . . . Yes . . . OK . . .

She turns off the phone in stunned shock.

They've found him.

Joyce　What?

Lia　Adam. He's turned up.

Joyce　What?

Lia　He's alive.

Her face breaks into an astonished smile. Blackout.

Scene Five

Lights up on a plain, bare airport waiting room.

Lia, *and* **Nick** *wait anxiously.* **Gordon** *comes in.*

Gordon　His plane landed five minutes ago. Joanna's going
to meet him and bring him straight in here. There's a media
scrum out there,

Lia　Maybe he won't know who we are. What if he doesn't
know who we are?

Nick　Well, we'll . . . deal with it.

Lia　I mean, how bad will it be? The memory thing?

Gordon　The consulate said he seemed physically OK.
Apart from a couple of stitches in his head.

Lia　I feel sick.

Gordon　The number of times I fantasised about him
coming back. I never imagined it like this.

Nick Deep breaths. Take deep breaths.

Lia Even if he can't remember anything, even if he doesn't know who we are, at least it's him. At least he'll smell of him. His skin, his hair, his eyes. I'll be able to kiss his face and it won't be dead. I was so frightened I'd never see his face again. I used to dream I'd get a skull in a box.

Nick Where the hell is he? Jesus Christ, I'm on the verge of a coronary here.

Joanna *appears, flustered, with large shoulder bag.*

Joanna Sorry. Sorry. His plane landed five minutes ago. Are you all OK?

Lia Thank you. We just need to see him now. We're all feeling sick.

Joanna I just want to ask you something and please feel free to say no, but it's just a small hand-held video camera –

She takes a camera from her bag.

Incredibly discreet, look you can hardly see it –

Lia No.

Joanna Fine.

Lia Sorry.

Gordon That's why we're in here. To get away from cameras.

Joanna Please, I understand.

Lia It's just –

Nick He's not in a good state.

Lia It's private.

Joanna I understand. Maybe we could do a reconstruction later? When you've all had a chance to, you know –

Lia I wish we could have spoken to him before he got on the plane.

Gordon   They said he wasn't terribly coherent. I told you.

Lia   D'you think it might have been a drug thing?

Gordon   Some sort of car crash, and he'd definitely been in hospital somewhere. I can't get anything else out of them.

Joanna *looks at her watch.*

Joanna   OK. He should be coming through by now. I'd better go and get him. It's incredible, isn't it? I've got butterflies in my stomach.

She goes out. Silence.

Lia   Is this real or are we dreaming it?

Nick   It's real.

Pause.

Lia   It doesn't feel right.

Gordon   We're anxious, that's all.

Lia   I want a cigarette. And I don't smoke. Maybe he'll have a beard.

Silence.

Nick   Or a tattoo.

Lia   Maybe he'll be covered in tattoos. Like the illustrated man.

They giggle slightly hysterically.

Silence.

Gordon   I don't think I can stand this much longer.

There's a knock at the door. They get up.

Lia   Yes?

It opens and **Joanna** *comes in, followed by a tall, red-haired boy, handsome, dishevelled, sheepish. He smiles at them uncertainly.*

Adam   Mum? Dad?

They stare at him. Silence.

Gordon   Who the fuck are you?

Lia *looks at* **Joanna** *in bewilderment.*

Lia   It's not him.

Blackout.

End of Act One.

Act Two

Scene One

Three days later.

Lia's *denuded study. Moonlit darkness.* **Lia** *is lying curled up in a chair in her pyjamas, with a blanket around her. She's staring into space.* **Nick** *comes in, carrying an overnight bag: he's been away.*

Nick What are you doing?

Lia *doesn't move.*

Lia Thinking. But I'm trying not to. How was the conference?

Nick Fine. Lia, upstairs, in the spare room −

Lia I don't want you to get in a state about it.

Nick How long has he been here?

Lia Since yesterday.

Nick Why? What the hell's going on?

Lia Where else is he supposed to go?

Nick He's not our responsibility.

Lia He can't stay in a hotel for ever.

Nick Does that mean he has to move in with us?

Lia It's temporary.

Nick He's disturbed. He should be in hospital.

Lia He's not disturbed. He's lost his memory and he doesn't know who he is.

Nick *puts a lamp on.*

Nick Look, he can't stay here. It's not −

Lia Not what?

Nick Healthy. We don't know who the fuck he is.

Lia Neither does he.

Nick That is not our problem.

Lia He thought we were his parents. He had the letters we sent to Adam. In his rucksack. He had Adam's plane tickets. His driving licence. He thought he was Adam. So did the consulate.

Nick How the hell did he get hold of this stuff?

Lia He doesn't know.

Nick He must.

Lia He doesn't.

Nick Well, make him remember.

Lia How? Torture him?

Nick Did Joanna ask you to take him in?

Lia No. It was my idea.

Nick Why?

Lia I just told you. He has nowhere else to go.

Nick He could be a criminal. He could be anything.

Lia We can't just do nothing.

Nick Lia. Whilst I admire your public spirit, can I just point out that there are proper organisations to deal with these sort of things.

Lia Such as?

Nick There are authorities.

Lia Authorities in charge of what? Amnesiacs?

Nick There are social workers.

Lia He needs somewhere to live. That's not a hospital or a hostel full of crack addicts.

Nick   He can't stay here!

'**Adam**' *appears in the doorway, sleepy, dressed in T-shirt and boxer shorts.*

Adam   I'm sorry. I didn't mean to cause trouble.

Lia   You're not. Really. You should go back to bed. You're supposed to get a lot of rest.

Adam   You were arguing about me.

Nick   How did you get hold of my son's things?

Adam   I don't know. They were in my backpack. I thought they were mine. I don't know why I've got them. I don't know where they came from.

Lia   They must have met each other somewhere.

Nick   This is ridiculous.

He goes out.

Lia   I'm sorry. He didn't know you were here.

Adam   I still don't really understand what's going on. I'm very confused.

Lia   In that, at least, you're not alone.

Adam   I'd like it to be sorted out.

Lia   It will be. You must have family somewhere.

Adam   I thought you were my family.

Lia   I'm sorry.

Nick *returns with a bottle of whisky and glasses. Slams them down on the desk, pours out three large ones. Hands them out.*

Nick   You'd better start at the beginning.

Lia   It's too late at night, Nick, and anyway, what beginning? He's lost his memory, there is none.

Adam   I speak English. I drink black coffee. I don't like sweet things. I do like dogs. That narrows it down a bit.

Nick How old are you?

Adam Obviously I'm not forty-five. I'm about, what – twenty?

Nick Where did you meet Adam?

Adam I don't even know if I did.

Nick So how have you got his stuff?

Lia You sound like the Gestapo. Stop it.

Adam I've no idea how I came to have it. I woke up in a hospital in Thailand. With no idea how I'd got there. And no idea who I was. And in my bag was all this stuff. So I went to the consulate. I thought I was Adam. But I'm not, am I?

Lia No.

Adam So who the fuck am I?

Nick You can't stay here. You need specialist treatment.

Adam OK. Right.

Pause.

You want me to go?

Lia No.

Nick Yes.

Adam What, right now?

Nick Yes.

Lia It's the middle of the night.

Adam I'll go. OK. It's just, I mean, like where?

Lia Please, just go back to bed. Get some sleep. Nick, he can't leave if he hasn't got anywhere to go to.

Nick That is not our problem. There are thousands of people on the streets with nowhere to go. Are we going to ask *them* to move in with us?

Adam   I don't know what you want me to do.

Lia   Go back to bed.

Nick   OK, I give up. Move in, why don't you?

Adam   So, I should . . . what?

Lia   Get some sleep.

Adam   Right. I'll, like, go back to bed, then. Thanks for the whisky.

Lia   Yes. Goodnight.

Adam   Goodnight. Thanks. Thanks for letting me stay. I really appreciate it.

He goes. When he gets to the door he turns.

D'you think they will find my real family?

Lia   I'm sure.

Adam   But if I don't know who I am, how will I recognise them?

Lia   I think your memory will gradually return.

Adam   How d'you know?

Lia   I don't, I'm just guessing.

Adam   I don't think I could live my entire life like this. I mean, it's weird. It's like not being real.

Pause.

I'm sorry about your son. If my memory comes back I might be able to tell you where I met him, mightn't I?

Lia   Yes.

Adam   That's if, like, I did meet him.

He goes. Blackout.

Scene Two

Garden bench. Day. It's hot. **Lia** *and* **Joanna**.

Joanna   It throws up a whole new set of possibilities.

Lia   It'd be a freak show.

Joanna   I've spoken to the broadcasters, we could get an hour-long slot.

Lia   No.

Joanna   But if Adam would agree –

Lia   Who?

Joanna   I'm sorry, I have to call him something. What do you call him?

Lia   Him. We call him 'him'.

Joanna   Maybe he'd like to do it. Someone will recognise him and he can be reunited with his family. That's what you want, isn't it?

Lia   Yes, of course –

Adam *appears eating an ice cream.*

Lia   D'you want to do this documentary or not?

Adam   I dunno.

Joanna   Someone's bound to recognise you. It would solve all your problems.

Adam   Some of them.

Lia   What happens to the programme about Adam?

Joanna   Obviously we'd link the two.

Lia   But it wouldn't really be about him any more.

Joanna   It would be about both of them.

Adam   I'm sorry. It just freaks me out, you know. I feel like something in a zoo.

Lia   Isn't it a bit exploitative?

Joanna   Oh, don't be ridiculous, I'm trying to help here.

Silence.

Sorry. I'm a bit stressed at the moment.

Lia   Why does everything have to be a television programme?

Joanna   Because that's what I do.

Adam   I don't want to do it just yet. If that's all right with you.

Joanna   Obviously you should take a little time to think about it.

Adam   OK.

Joanna   I wouldn't want to push you before you're ready.

Adam   OK.

Joanna   But they're very serious about commissioning this.

Adam   Maybe in a while. Do the programme you originally intended. Forget about me for now.

Lia   Everyone seems to have forgotten about Adam. Except me.

Joanna   No, Lia, that's not true – (*To* **Adam**.) But you're completely bound up with it. It's an incredible story. We could get a huge audience. ABC1s.

Lia   At the start of all this, I thought you wanted to find Adam. Then I suspected you just needed to make a buck. Now I see it's actually about bloody ratings. This is what my son's become.

Joanna   But there's no point doing it without an audience.

Lia   I'm not sure there's any point doing it, period.

She goes.

Joanna   Fuck.

Silence.

Adam   I shouldn't be here.

Joanna   Maybe we should find somewhere else for you to stay.

Adam   I think she wants me here. I don't know why.

Joanna   You've just said you shouldn't be here.

Adam   It'd be worse if I left now. She thinks I'm going to lead her to him.

Joanna   Are you?

Adam   She showed me a photograph and it didn't mean a thing to me. It could have been anyone.

Joanna   You look a bit like him. Did you see the resemblance?

Adam   I suppose that's why they gave me the passport.

Joanna   It's actually quite freaky. Even though I've only seen a photo of him.

Adam   D'you think she can see it?

Joanna   Yeah.

Adam   So I'm kind of Adam lite.

Joanna   Although maybe you look a bit older. How d'you find out someone's age? D'you look at their teeth?

Adam   Why don't you cut off my legs and count the rings?

Joanna   I think you're about twenty-three or four.

Adam   Don't worry about the programme. I will do it. I just don't want to upset her, you know? She wanted it to be about Adam, and now it's going to be about me.

Joanna   Well, not entirely.

Adam   You just have to be a bit sensitive, that's all.

Joanna   OK. So you're saying you will do it?

Adam   Yeah. Eventually. When the time is right.

Pause.

Joanna   You're very protective of her.

Adam   I like her. She's been really kind.

Joanna   What about him?

Adam   He's OK. He was freaked at first.

Joanna   You're quite a strange creature, aren't you?

Adam   Totally fucking weird. So would you be if you didn't know your own name.

Joanna   Did they book an appointment with the shrink?

Adam   Yeah. Next week sometime. And a neurologist. To find out if I have brain injuries.

Joanna   Good . . . Good.

A beat.

I just want to ask you something and please feel free to say no –

She takes out her video camera.

It's incredibly discreet, you'll hardly notice it's there. I mean obviously not in the actual consultation, but maybe in the waiting room, and coming out afterwards –

Adam   Sure.

Joanna   Great. Thank you so much.

Adam   That's OK.

Joanna   I'm so pissed off I didn't get the moment when Gordon said 'Who the fuck are you?' at the airport.

Adam   Yes you did, I saw you.

Joanna   What?

Adam   Your bag had a hole in it.

Joanna   No, it didn't.

Adam   You filmed me coming through arrivals. Then you put the camera in your bag. Which had a hole in. And you kept filming.

A beat. She looks at him. She knows that he knows.

Joanna   Look, it's very complicated.

Adam   Sure.

Joanna   I promise you, I did it for the best possible reasons.

Adam   OK.

Joanna   It didn't come out terribly well anyway.

Adam   Right.

Joanna   The point is, we have to keep people watching. If they turn off, the whole thing's a waste of time.

Adam   I understand, don't worry.

Joanna   I'd rather you didn't say anything about it for now.

Adam   Won't they like, spot it, when the programme comes out?

Joanna   It's too late to do anything about it by then.

Adam   Cool.

Joanna   But you don't mind me filming you, do you?

Adam   Why should I? I'm no one. I don't exist. I've no past. Which means, like, no scruples and no conscience. I'm fucked. Nothing you do can make it any worse.

Joanna   Can I take some photos of you?

Adam   Now?

Joanna   Yeah.

Adam   Why?

Joanna   Publicity shots.

Adam   Why don't you get a photographer to do them?

Joanna   That's what I started out as. A photographer.

Adam   I don't like having my photo taken.

Joanna   How d'you know?

Adam   You don't really understand memory loss, do you?

Joanna   No. Do you?

Joanna has taken out her camera.

Adam   I get self-conscious.

Joanna   Just keep talking and you won't notice what I'm doing. Tell me about yourself.

She takes a photo. He looks uncomfortable.

Adam   I don't like honey. I discovered that yesterday.

Joanna   Really? Look this way more. Where did you meet Adam?

Adam   I told you, I've no idea. Or if I even did.

Joanna   You need to look blanker than that. Try and look a bit bewildered.

Adam   Like this?

Joanna   Yeah, great.

She fires off more photos.

What about going to a hypnotist? How would you feel about that?

Adam   Why?

Joanna   They might be able to take you back to before the accident.

Adam OK. Cool. I don't mind.

She takes another shot.

Joanna When you turned up at the consulate, what did you say?

Adam I said I was Adam Kilmartin and I'd lost my passport, blah, blah, blah. I was a bit confused. But they were really pleased to see me. This woman gave me a cake. I was caught up in the whirl of it. I felt high. I thought my problems were over. And then I got back here and it was all a mistake.

Joanna So why didn't the people in the hospital get in touch with the consulate?

Adam I asked them that and they said they couldn't find my papers. But you know, they were in my bag, in a side pocket. I don't know how they could have missed them.

Pause.

Joanna What d'you think your real parents are like?

Adam No idea.

She takes another photo.

D'you think photographs lie?

Joanna Yeah. All the time.

Adam Have you got enough?

Joanna Yeah. Thanks.

She puts down the camera.

Adam I've told you about me. Now tell me something about you.

Joanna I was born in Surrey. I'm twenty-eight years old.

Adam And you've already got kids? Cool.

Joanna Who told you that?

Adam   Lia. She said you keep saying 'As a mother myself'.

Joanna   You have to get people on your side. You have to find common ground.

Adam   Right.

Joanna   I am going to have kids at some point in my life.

Adam   But you haven't got any at the moment?

A beat.

Joanna   No.

Adam   That's OK. That's cool.

Joanna   Sometimes you have to tell white lies. That's perfectly permissible in pursuit of the truth.

Adam   You're quite cute aren't you?

Joanna   Cute-gorgeous or cute-devious?

Adam   Which would you prefer?

Joanna   Oh, I think the former.

Adam   Would you like to fuck me?

Joanna   Probably. But I never mix business with pleasure.

Adam   You sound like an air hostess.

Joanna   D'you know many air hostesses?

Adam   Not as far as I'm aware.

Joanna   So what exactly is going on in your brain?

Adam   It's hard to describe.

Joanna   Try me.

Adam   I don't know who I am but everything else is in perfect working order.

Joanna   Meaning?

Adam   I think you're very attractive.

Joanna   I'm flattered.

Adam   Are you really twenty-eight?

Joanna   No. I'm thirty-three.

Adam   I'm good at spotting lies.

Joanna   I said I was twenty-eight so I'd be closer to your age so you might think I was more attractive.

Adam   So why won't you fuck me?

Joanna   I told you.

Adam   I brought you a present.

He takes a small tissue-paper package from his pocket and gives it to her. She opens it. A pair of earrings.

Joanna   They're beautiful.

Adam   Are they?

Joanna   Where did you get them from?

Adam   Shall I tell you the truth?

Joanna   Yeah.

Adam   They were at the bottom of my rucksack. In a little leather pouch. So I didn't, like, buy them or anything. Sorry.

Joanna   And you don't know where they came from, apart from that?

Adam   No. But, I mean, they're not much use to me are they?

She puts them on.

Joanna   What d'you think?

He leans over and kisses her, long and deep. Blackout.

Scene Three

Garden. It's hot. **Adam** *is lying on a rug reading.* **Lia** *comes out.*

Adam Hi.

He turns over. He's wearing a Coldplay T-shirt.

Lia That's Adam's T-shirt.

Adam What?

Lia That's Adam's.

Adam What is?

Lia You're wearing his T-shirt.

Adam It's not his T-shirt, it's mine.

Lia It was in his room. What were you doing in his room?

Adam I wasn't. I don't know what you're talking about.

Lia The T-shirt was in his room.

Adam You mean he has one the same as this?

Lia No, that *is* his.

Adam It's not, but look, there, I'll take it off –

He takes it off. His torso is covered in scars.

Lia Oh. Oh my God. What happened?

Adam I think it must have been the car crash.

Lia I'm sorry.

Adam It doesn't hurt or anything. You can touch it if you like. Look –

He takes her hand and moves it towards the scars. She pulls her hand away.

Lia That's all right.

Adam It's kind of numb. I've got no feeling there. Here.

He hands her the T-shirt.

Lia   Please. It doesn't matter.

Adam   I don't want to wear it if it upsets you.

Lia   Are you sure it's yours?

Adam   It was in my bag, so I'm presuming it's mine. Although fuck knows, it could be anyone's. You've got me really confused now.

Lia   You didn't take it from his room?

Adam   No.

Lia   Maybe it wasn't in his room. I can't remember where it was now.

Adam   Look, as far as I know, this is my T-shirt.

Lia   So you like Coldplay then?

Adam   I don't know. I suppose I must do. It's not that unusual is it?

Lia   No. I suppose not. I'm sorry. Please, put it back on.

Adam   I don't want to wear it if it's the same as one of Adam's. It doesn't feel right.

Lia   Please. It's just a T-shirt.

A beat.

Adam   OK.

He puts it back on.

I feel really uncomfortable now.

Lia   You look a bit like him.

Adam   Adam?

Lia   It's quite . . . spooky.

Adam   D'you want to, like, talk about him?

Lia I don't know how to start.

Adam Anywhere.

Lia I won't know where to finish.

Adam I'm not going anywhere.

Lia D'you have a cigarette?

Adam No. People of your age aren't supposed to smoke.

Lia I'm experimenting.

Adam Did Adam smoke?

Lia He said he didn't, but he did.

Adam What did he look like?

Lia Tall. Reddish hair, like yours. Beautiful. Obviously.

Adam And you think I look a bit like him? I'm flattered.

Lia There's something. A look.

Adam If this was a bad movie I'd be his long-lost twin and I'd have turned up to claim you as my mother.

Lia You're not identical.

Adam No. Obviously. That would be too weird for words.

Lia And now you're sitting in our garden wearing his T-shirt and the world's turned upside down.

Adam It's not his T-shirt.

Lia No. I'm sorry.

Pause.

D'you think you did meet him somewhere? In Indonesia? Or Australia?

Adam I must have, mustn't I? Otherwise how have I got his stuff?

Lia You're the last connection we have with him. You're where the trail runs out.

Adam   I don't know what to say.

Lia   It's not your fault. I'm sorry.

A beat.

Adam   Can I just say something?

Lia   What?

Adam   I don't trust Joanna.

Lia   My father says she has an unfortunate manner, but she's basically sound.

Adam   You should be more wary of her.

Lia   What d'you mean 'wary'?

Adam   She films stuff with a hidden camera.

Lia   Like what?

Adam   Like when you met me at the airport.

Lia   We asked her not to.

Adam   Well, she did.

Lia   How d'you know?

Adam   Because I saw her. I thought you must have known.

Lia   Have you spoken to her about it?

Adam   Yeah. She said it didn't come out. So don't worry, there's no footage. But we should be careful, that's all.

Lia   I'd rather not have anything more to do with her.

Adam   Thing is, it's my only chance.

Lia   Of what?

Adam   Finding out who I am. If, like millions of people see it.

Lia   But if she's dishonest –

Adam   Yeah, but we're one-up on her because we know that. And she doesn't know we know.

Lia   She knows you do.

Adam   I told her I wouldn't tell you.

Pause.

Lia   I just want to know what happened to my son.

Adam   And I just want to know who I am.

Lia   D'you honestly think Joanna wants to help either of us?

Adam   Yeah. Weirdly, I think she does. It's all a bit muddled up with her own ambition, that's all. But nobody's motives are pure. There's always a whole load of other shit going on. Don't you think?

Lia   I don't know. I don't know anything any more. Except you look so like Adam standing there.

Adam   I'm sorry. It's the T-shirt. I won't wear it again, I promise.

Lia   You never told us what the doctor said.

Adam   The shrink?

Lia   Yes.

Adam   You know shrinks. They never say anything.

Lia   Don't they?

Adam   They just listen and say mmmm.

Lia   So you've seen one before?

Adam   I don't think so. But I've read a lot of books. And this one confirmed everything I've ever read.

Lia   Which is what?

Adam   They're a waste of time.

Lia   So you won't be going back.

Adam   Not unless you want me to.

Lia   I think you need to get to the bottom of it.

Adam   The bottom of what?

Lia   Why you lost your memory.

Adam   OK. If it makes you happy, I'll keep going.

Lia   You don't have to do it for me. Do it for you.

Adam   I'd rather do it for you. I mean, like, I ought to do something, don't you think? I can't just take and take and give nothing back, can I?

Lia   It really is up to you.

Pause.

But you will keep seeing the neurologist, won't you?

Adam   Yeah, that's different.

Lia   How?

Adam   It's empirical. He looks at my brain and tells me what's missing. He doesn't ask me stupid questions and then hazard a guess.

Lia   You prefer facts to conjecture?

Adam   Every time. Don't you?

Lia   All I've got is conjecture.

Adam   Sorry. I know.

Pause.

I'm going to go and take this T-shirt off. It's making me self-conscious.

Lia   OK.

He goes out. **Lia** *picks up the book he was reading. Looks at the cover.*

Hey!

But he's gone. Blackout.

Scene Four

Lia's study. It's hot. **Joyce Tindle** *and* **Nick**. **Nick** *is looking at his watch.*

Nick   She said she'd be back around four. Are you sure I can't get you a cup of tea?

Joyce   What I'd really like is to plunge naked into a bath full of ice.

Nick   Right.

A beat.

Failing that, what about tea?

Joyce   You're not very keen on me are you, dear? But you're too polite to say.

Nick   I can't say I have any particular feelings about you.

Joyce   It's an English thing. Never say what you mean.

Nick   I'm not actually English.

Joyce   And that's another English thing, dear. Never admit you actually *are* English. I expect you're Scottish or Welsh or Irish are you?

Nick   Scots-Irish.

Joyce   Three generations ago.

Nick   Two.

Joyce   You're very resistant, Nick.

Nick   To what?

Joyce   Almost everything. It's making you ill.

Nick   I'm not ill.

Joyce   When was the last time you went to the doctor?

Nick   Three months ago.

Joyce And what did he say?

Nick That's none of your business.

Joyce He said you should stop grinding your teeth. It's giving you headaches.

Nick I don't grind my teeth.

Joyce You're doing it now.

Nick Look, if you don't want tea, I'm going to have to be very rude and leave you to it –

Joyce Milk, no sugar. Don't bother to make a whole pot. A mug will do.

He goes out. **Joyce** *looks round the room. Glances at the papers on* **Lia***'s desk. Finds the tennis ball contraption, and picks it up, examines it, puzzled.* **Nick** *comes back with a glass of water.*

Nick Sorry, we're out of tea.

She holds the contraption.

Joyce What's this?

Nick You tell me, you're the psychic.

Joyce I refuse to rise to the bait.

Nick Adam made it.

Joyce I thought so.

Nick You would.

Joyce You're so angry I can feel it. It's like someone running their fingers down a blackboard.

Nick And now you're going to tell me to let it all out, and get in touch with my feelings.

Joyce That's the sort of thing they say in womens' magazines, dear. It's got nothing to do with what I do.

Nick Which is what?

Joyce   The boy you have staying with you. He's very troubled.

Nick   We're aware of that.

Joyce   More than you realise. He's a lost soul.

Nick   Thank you for sharing that with me.

Joyce   You don't speak from your heart any more. It's just reflex, isn't it?

Nick   Look, I didn't ask you here, Lia did –

Joyce   She didn't actually. I came because I needed to speak with her.

Nick   Well, she's not in, so if you don't mind I'm going to leave you while I get on with some work.

Joyce   All right, dear.

He starts to go.

Your mother says it was an accident. She didn't mean to take them.

He turns round.

Nick   What?

Joyce   I think she's saying she got her sleeping tablets muddled. Does that mean anything to you?

Nick   She took an overdose.

Joyce   Well, she's saying it was an accident.

Nick   Where d'you get this information from?

Joyce   Your mother. I've got her in my left ear. She's very happy.

Nick   You never get anyone who's miserable, do you?

Joyce   Death is transcendent.

Nick   You never get anyone saying I regret it all, it's all shit, there's no redemption, life's a bitch and death's worse.

Joyce   Because it's not like that.

Nick   D'you get people who've been blown to pieces saying hey, it's all great, I'm really glad I was blown to bits or burnt to death or I had to jump out of that window onto the street three miles below, I'm glad I went splat on the pavement because now I'm skipping around on clouds having one hell of a good time?

Joyce   In death there is no more pain and no more crying.

Nick   What? For anyone? So the fuckers who blew up my son are at the party too? Where's the fucking sense in that?

Joyce   Why are you so sure Adam was blown up?

Nick   Maybe they're all sitting around now with a few beers saying hey, no hard feelings, we didn't mean it personally, but you know, now you're dead, we realise you're actually a very nice person and guess what? So are we!

Joyce   You don't know he was blown up, do you?

Nick   I'm speaking hypothetically.

Joyce   Your mother says you need to take up something calming. Like yoga.

Nick   My mother wouldn't know yoga from water polo.

Joyce   Oh, she does now. Ashtanga. She's very fit.

Nick   My mother's doing yoga in the netherworld? Are you insane?

Lia *comes in.*

Lia   Oh, Joyce. I wasn't expecting you. How long have you been here?

Nick   She says my mother's taken up yoga.

Lia   Your mother's dead.

Nick   Dead, alive, what's the difference? It's all lovely. Everything's fucking lovely all the fucking time in her world.

Lia　I need to speak to you.

Nick　Alone?

Lia　I don't know, maybe I'm going mad.

Nick　What's happened?

Joyce　It's the boy isn't it?

Lia　All the stuff that was going to charity. The books and stuff. I think he's been opening the boxes He was reading one of the books. And two of the paintings are on the wall in his room.

Nick　It doesn't make much sense. It's not even surreptitious. Why would he do that?

Joyce　Why don't you ask him?

Nick　Why don't you know?

Joyce　Because I'm not a psychiatrist.

Nick　Is he in?

Lia　He's upstairs. (*She goes and shouts, off.*) Are you up there? D'you think you could come down here a minute?

Adam (*off*)　OK.

Lia　What are we going to say to him?

Nick　Just ask him.

Lia　What?

Nick　Oh for fuck's sake, I'll do it.

Adam *appears.*

Adam　Hi.

Nick　We were just wondering –

Lia　– about the book you were reading.

Adam　What book?

Lia   The one you were reading in the garden.

Adam   Oh, right. What about it?

Nick   You took it from one of the parcels upstairs.

Adam   No I didn't.

Lia   The box was opened and the tape was cut.

Adam   It was already like that. I'm sorry. Are they precious or something? Was I not supposed to read them? I'm sorry. I didn't realise.

Lia   No, it's not that, it's just −

Nick   Somebody opened the parcel.

Adam   Well, it wasn't me.

Joyce   And the paintings in your bedroom, dear.

Adam   What paintings?

Lia   You must have taken them from the box.

Adam   I don't even know what you're talking about.

Lia   They're on the wall in his room, I saw them.

Nick   OK, it's easy to settle.

He goes out.

Adam   I don't know what it is I'm supposed to have done.

Lia   It's not a crime or anything, I just think you could have asked.

Adam   Asked what?

Lia   If you could have the paintings. Or borrow them or something.

Adam   What do they look like, these paintings?

Lia   You know what they look like. They're on the wall next to your bed.

Adam Maybe I've just never noticed them.

Lia No. You put them there –

Nick *reappears.*

Nick I can't see them.

Lia What?

Nick They're not there.

Adam I told you.

Nick All the paintings are in a box on the landing.

Lia But they were on the wall, I saw them.

Nick When?

Lia Just now. Ten minutes ago.

Nick Well, they're not there now.

Adam Because they never were.

Lia I'm not imagining this.

Adam What were you doing in my room?

Lia What?

Adam What were you doing in there?

Lia I was . . .

Adam D'you think I'm a thief or something?

Lia No. I was going to straighten things up.

Adam It doesn't need straightening up.

Lia No, I realise that –

Adam Why would I steal your paintings?

Lia I'm sorry, I just . . . I was sure I saw them.

Nick Look, this has all been a bit of a misunderstanding. Lia's under a lot of strain, things are very difficult for us all at the moment. I'm sorry.

A beat.

Adam Yeah, OK. I'm sorry too. I'm sorry I lost my rag with you. Let's just forget it, shall we?

Lia I'm sorry. I must be going mad.

Adam You're not. It's just . . .

Lia What?

Adam Maybe, I don't know, you should see a doctor or something?

Lia Yes.

Adam I'm sorry for not being more understanding.

He goes over and hugs **Lia**. *She's taken aback.*

Adam I know it's horrible for you at the moment. I wish I could make it better but I don't know what to do.

Lia It's OK. Honestly.

Adam *starts to cry.*

Adam (*crying*) I just feel lost. Like I'm on a raft in the middle of the sea and it's night and I don't know where I am or how I got here or where I'm going or if I'll make it.

Lia Please. It's OK.

Adam I feel stupid now. I'm sorry.

He rushes from the room. Pause.

Joyce He's not sorry.

Nick Is that you being psychic or just a wild guess?

Joyce He didn't really explain the book, did he?

Lia I don't know. I give up. It's obviously not him. It's me. Maybe I'm losing my grip on reality.

Joyce No dear, it's him. That's what I wanted to say to you. Everyone has an aura, you know that, don't you? Yours is clouded by grief, but it's still sympathetic. His is very dark, and clotted. When he leaves you'll need to spring clean the house.

Blackout.

Scene Five

Lia's study. Next day.

Adam is sitting at **Lia**'s desk, smoking and reading through her notes. There's a glass of wine at his elbow. **Lia** comes in.

Adam   This is really interesting.

Lia   What are you doing?

Adam   This woman going to India to find her son. And becoming a Hindu.

Lia   Buddhist. Give those to me.

Adam   If you sit, just sit. If you walk, just walk. Don't wobble.

Lia   What?

Adam   Buddhist haiku.

Lia   I really don't think you should be in here.

Adam   Oh, I'm sorry. She's interesting, though, isn't she, this Frances Hewer?

Lia   You shouldn't be reading that.

Adam   Do you feel some kind of bond, because her son was killed?

Lia   No.

Adam   I would.

Lia   This is nothing to do with you.

Adam   What was he doing there anyway? In India?

Lia   It was part of the empire.

Adam   So they sent him out to do a bit of colonising. And then the bastard natives hacked him to bits. They don't like it when we mess with their culture, do they?

Lia   You shouldn't just walk in here. It's my room.

Adam   You walked into mine.

Lia   It's my house.

Adam   OK. I'm sorry.

Pause.

If I was a bit older, and you were a bit younger, would you fancy me?

Lia   That's really not an appropriate question.

Adam   No, but I mean. If I look like Adam, I must look like his dad.

Lia   You don't.

Adam   Go on. Look at me again. Can you see it?

Lia   No –

Adam   Where did you meet him? Was it a one-night stand?

The phone rings. **Adam** *picks it up.*

Hello? . . . She is . . . Who's calling, please?

He hands the phone to **Lia**

It's for you.

Lia   Hello?

She listens.

Didn't he? . . . I'm so sorry . . . I'll speak to him . . . Thank you.

She puts the phone down.

That was the psychiatrist.

Adam   I know.

Lia   You didn't go to any of the appointments.

Adam   No.

Lia   You told me you did.

Adam   I didn't want to disappoint you.

Lia   You told me you would keep going because I wanted you to.

Adam   I don't think I actually said that, did I?

Lia   Yes.

Adam   Well, I'm sorry. I failed you.

Lia   Did you keep the appointment with the neurologist?

Adam   Yes.

Lia   You're lying, aren't you?

He begins to giggle.

Adam   I can't remember.

Lia   Why didn't you go?

Adam   I don't know. I feel like a freak. I don't like doctors.

Lia   We went to all this trouble sorting it out for you –

Adam   Oh, excuse me.

Lia   What?

Adam   It's your house, it's your room, I'm not supposed to be in here, I'm stealing your paintings, and now I'm not grateful enough –

Lia   That's not what I said.

Adam   You fancy yourself as a bit of a saint, don't you?

Lia   I don't know what you mean.

He picks up some pieces of paper from her desk, reads.

Adam   'The Duality of Goodness – what one culture may perceive as evil, another may perceive as good. Or at least a necessary step on a trajectory towards ultimate good. Open brackets, Bombing civilians, close brackets – '

Lia   Give that to me –

Adam   'The possibility: Adam killed by someone who saw it as a "good" action. Goodness as an elusive chimera. Changing with the light. Slippery as a shadow.' Have you thought of writing a book of poetry? *Trite Titles for the New Millennium?*

Lia   Stop it –

She tries to take it from him, but he swerves away.

Adam   Hang on – 'Goodness as denial of self? Suicide bombers. Goodness out of evil. Is this possible? Do no harm. Do no harm. Is that what it boils down to? Is it as simple as that?' Fuck me.

Lia   Give that to me!

Adam   Seven out of ten for trying. But you know, what I always say is, scratch a secular saint and there's always a nasty little bourgeois cunt underneath.

Lia   Get out.

Adam   Whoops. Said the 'c' word.

Lia   Are you drunk?

Adam   Rat-arsed.

He grins and slumps on the desk. **Gordon** *comes in.*

Hi!

Gordon   Hello.

Adam *sits up.*

Adam   We're just having a discussion about the impossibility of goodness in an imperfect world.

He takes another swig of wine and **Lia** *takes the glass from him.*

Lia   OK, that's enough –

Adam   Ahhh, Mum . . .

Gordon   Bit early for drinking isn't it?

Adam   Hey, you'd drink if you were in my position.

Gordon   Don't you think it's about time you moved out?

Adam   I'm sorry I'm being a burden on you all.

Gordon   That's putting it mildly.

Adam   I can't help it, I'm a man without a past, and with fuck-all future as far as I can see.

Lia   I'm sorry. I take you in, I feed you, I even give you money. And in return you behave like you own the place and call me a cunt

Adam   Oh, pardon me, Lady Bountiful –

Lia   You're drunk, go away and sober up –

Adam   Give me my wine back .

Gordon   Look, you little shit –

Lia   Just get out, will you?

Adam   Oooh, fuck, I've really riled her now.

He gets up and goes to the door. **Lia** *watches him.*

Lia   Hey.

Adam   What?

Lia   That's Nick's shirt.

Adam   Oh, for Christ's sake. It's not Nick's shirt, it's mine.

Lia   No, it's not.

Adam   Bloody hell. It's just an ordinary blue shirt. And it belongs to me. That's why I'm wearing it.

Lia   I know it's Nick's because I bought it for him.

Adam   I don't know what you're talking about. It's mine. I bought it in Selfridges, OK?

Lia   How d'you know you bought it in Selfridges?

Adam   Because that's what it says on the label? D'you want to look?

A beat.

Lia   No. No. It's OK. Fine, it's yours, I made a mistake.

Adam   Thank you.

He goes out.

Gordon   *Is* it Nick's shirt?

Lia   I thought it was. But you can't stand there all day going oh-yes-it-is, oh-no-it-isn't. You feel so stupid.

Gordon   Damaged goods.

Lia   What?

Gordon   Him.

Lia   He was in an accident.

Gordon   How do we know that?

Lia   He's covered in scars.

Gordon   Get rid of him. Tell him to bugger off.

Lia   Maybe we've been expecting too much of him.

Gordon   Joanna should sort it out. She got you into it.

Lia   He's drunk, that's all.

Gordon   In vino veritas. If he's an arsehole when he's drunk, he's an arsehole, period.

Lia   He's got me so confused.

Gordon   Lia, this kid is bad news. Everything about him screams fuck-up.

Lia   He was sitting in my chair, going through my papers.

Gordon   Are you listening to me?

Lia   I'm trying to give him the benefit of the doubt.

Gordon   Why?

Lia   Because something bad has obviously happened to him −

Gordon   Something bad has happened to all of us. We've lost Adam. And got this prick instead.

Lia   But he might be able to lead us to Adam.

Gordon   He hasn't shown any inclination to do anything of the sort so far.

Lia   He's the only link we've got to him. And anyway, when he's sober he's OK −

She's aware of the glass of wine in her hand. Something about it disturbs her. She sniffs it.

Gordon   What?

Lia   What does that smell like to you?

Gordon *takes it and sniffs it.*

Gordon   Ribena?

He tastes it.

It's Ribena.

Blackout.

Scene Six

Same room. Night.

Adam *is sitting in **Lia**'s desk chair, in the dark, wrapped in a blanket. There's a half-empty bottle of whisky in front of him. The light flicks on. **Lia**, **Nick** and **Gordon** come in.*

Nick   Look, this isn't really working out.

Adam   What?

Nick   You're going to have to leave.

Adam   What d'you mean?

Lia   We've spoken to Joanna, and she says you can go and stay with her for a while.

Adam   Why? What have I done?

Nick *holds up a blue shirt.*

Nick   This is my shirt. It was in your room.

Adam   You're throwing me out because I borrowed a fucking shirt?

Lia   Stop it, you know that isn't it.

Adam   I can't stay with Joanna. I hate her. I can't stand her.

Gordon   Yes, well, we hate you, so hard luck.

Adam   Explain to me what it is I'm supposed to have done.

Lia   I'm sorry. I'm not in a very good state at the moment and I shouldn't have invited you to stay. I'm not blaming you, it was my fault.

Adam   You don't think that for a fucking minute.

Nick   Listen, we're not having an argument about this. Joanna's coming to pick you up. That's it

Adam   Please don't make me go. Please. I want to stay here. I feel like I've got a family when I'm with you.

Gordon   Unfortunately we're not your family.

Adam   I'm sorry. I'm sorry I've been weird, I don't understand what's going on inside my head.

Gordon   Neither do we, and we've given up trying.

Adam   I don't understand what it is I'm supposed to have done.

Nick   Joanna'll be here in five minutes. Go and pack your stuff.

Adam   I can't stay with her. She's a fucking sociopath. D'you know she hasn't actually got any children? She just made it up.

Lia   That's neither here nor there.

Adam   D'you want to know what she said about you?

Lia   No.

Adam   She said she's not surprised Adam disappeared, you're so fucking neurotic you'd have driven anyone away.

Gordon   All right, that's enough.

Adam   She said that. How can you send me to stay with her?

Gordon   We've done our best, now it's her turn.

Adam   Just tell me what crime I'm supposed to have committed?

Lia   I want you to leave. That's all.

Adam   Why?

Lia   It's my house and I don't want you here! I don't have to tell you why!

Adam   Oh, now the worm turns. Oh, I'm such a good, decent person, I can see the good in everyone, I'm so fucking caring, I'm practically Mother Teresa. But only up to a point. Everyone has to draw the line somewhere, don't they?

Nick   Get your stuff and go.

Adam *starts to cry.*

Adam   Sorry. I'm sorry. I didn't mean it. I don't know why I say this stuff, I can't help it. Please don't make me go. Please. I'll see the shrink. I'll see anyone.

Lia It's no good. I can't cope with you. I'm sorry.

Adam   OK.

He gets up slowly, still wrapped in the blanket.

I'll go then.

He crosses the room, and as he does so, there's a pinging sound as a razor blade hits the floor. Blood splashes onto the floor as he walks.

Oh, Jesus Christ . . .

Adam *drops the blanket: he's wearing only a pair of underpants, and he's cut both his arms in a criss cross pattern from shoulder to wrists. There's also a huge slash across his chest and stomach. Blood streams as he stands in the centre of the room, crying.*

Blackout.

Scene Seven

Same room. Next Day.

Lia *is sitting at her desk, staring into space, smoking.* **Adam** *comes in. His arms are bandaged, but he looks calm.*

Adam   Can I come in?

Lia   You've done it before, haven't you?

Adam   What?

Lia   Cut yourself.

Adam   I don't remember.

Lia   Oh, fuck that amnesia shit.

Adam   I might have done it before. I honestly don't know.

Lia   You're covered in old scars. They're not from a car accident. You knew exactly how deep to cut. The wounds are superficial. That's what the doctors said.

Adam   I'm sorry.

Lia   That doesn't change anything.

Adam   I'm sorry.

Lia   Stop saying sorry. You don't mean it.

Adam   How do you know?

Lia   You're only here because the hospital insisted. Not because we want you here.

Adam   OK.

Lia   So when are you leaving?

Adam   I don't know, I haven't thought.

Lia   So think.

Pause.

Adam   I didn't mean those things I said last night.

Lia   You remember them, do you?

Adam   Of course I do.

Lia   What else do you remember?

Adam   What d'you mean?

Lia   Who are you?

Adam   I don't know.

Lia   Did you make anonymous phone calls to us?

Adam   No.

Lia   Call and then put the phone down? We know you had our number.

Adam   No.

Lia   I don't believe you.

Adam   I said terrible things to you, and I don't know why I said them, because I don't think them. But I never called you, I promise. This stuff comes out of my mouth and it

doesn't feel like me. It feels like someone else is saying it.
If they say I've cut myself before, then I must have done,
but I don't remember it. I'm sorry I can't tell you who I am
because I honestly don't know. And I'm sorry I keep saying
sorry, but I am.

Lia   How did you get my son's stuff, that's all I want to
know.

Adam   I've told you, I've no idea –

Joanna *comes in.*

Joanna   I've booked you into a hotel.

Adam   I'm not allowed to be on my own.

Lia   You're not my responsibility.

Adam   The doctor said I shouldn't be left alone.

Joanna   You can't stay here.

Adam   Why not?

Joanna   You know why not. Come on.

Adam   I don't want to go.

Joanna   What am I supposed to do?

Lia   I don't know. Shoot him?

Adam   I actually feel a whole lot better that I did
yesterday.

Lia   So. No chance you might cut your throat, then?

Adam   It was just a cry for help.

Lia *looks at* **Joanna**

Lia   Did he give you those earrings?

Joanna *touches her ears.*

Joanna   These? Yes.

Lia   They're mine.

Joanna   Oh God . . . I'm so sorry.

She takes them off and hands them back to **Lia**.

Adam   I didn't give her them. What the fuck is she talking about?

Joanna   You said you found them in your rucksack.

Adam   When?

Joanna   When you gave them to me!

Adam   No. Let's just be clear about this. Let's be rational and calm, and hey, why not, let's be truthful for once. Let's get the facts straight. You took the earrings from Lia's bedroom. That's what you told me. You put them on, and said, 'What d'you think of these? I nicked them.'

Joanna   I did not!

Adam   OK. So where did you get them? Because it wasn't from me.

Joanna   I didn't take them, honestly, I don't know why he's saying this.

Adam   I might have lost my memory but I'm not a thief.

Joanna   He said he found them in his rucksack.

Lia   He just says the first thing that comes into his head. Haven't you realised that?

Joanna   You sick shit.

Adam   Excuse me. You lied about having kids. You lied about your age. You said you only fucked her father, but actually you also fucked her husband.

Joanna   What?

Adam   And I'm sorry I had to bring that up, Lia, but it's true.

Joanna   It is not! What else can I say? It's not. I hardly – I don't even –

Adam You told me yourself. You said sometimes you have to lie to get what you want. And you said her son was a swotty little faggot.

Joanna *reels in astonishment.*

Joanna What?

Adam That's what you said.

Joanna Fuck you. You're insane. I wash my hands of you. Lia, I'm sorry, none of this is true, none of it –

Adam What? *None* of it?

Joanna There's your hotel reservation.

She throws down some papers.

Three nights are paid for. After that you're on your own. Lia, I'm sorry, but I'm out of here. If I were you I'd call the police. Everything he's just said is horseshit. Everything. I didn't say any of those things. I'll call you.

She goes.

Lia You're quite scary, aren't you?

Adam She did say that stuff.

Lia And you thought I ought to know?

Adam *has been looking at the tennis-ball contraption. He deftly changes the subject.*

Adam Is that what I think it is?

Lia What?

He goes and picks it up.

Adam How does it work?

Lia Adam made it.

Adam Show me how it works.

Lia It's just a thing that fires tennis balls. I don't know what purpose it serves.

Adam Show me.

Lia No.

Adam OK.

He goes to the machine, sets it up and fires the tennis balls. He watches.

Wow. And you don't know what it's for?

Lia It isn't for anything. It's just something he made when he was thirteen.

Adam It's fairly crude. So you calibrate the thing as precisely as you can, fire the balls at exactly the same moment on completely level ground.

He fires the machine again. The balls bounce across the stage.

No wind, no external interference of any kind. At least none that you can measure. And the balls start off in sync, but they always, eventually, bounce out of sync.

Lia Meaning?

Adam Tiny, unforeseen things happen. Tiny shifts in atmosphere, minute differentials in calibration. They all have an effect that we can't measure because we can't see them. You can't predict when or how an event will occur. You can only predict the likelihood of an event occurring. It's the theory of non-locality.

Lia How d'you know this?

She picks up the machine protectively and puts it on her desk.

Adam It's exactly like he said.

Lia Like who said?

Adam Adam.

Lia What?

Adam He told me he made this when he was a kid.

A beat.

Lia   You met him?

Adam   How d'you think I've got his stuff?

Lia   But you said you didn't know how you came to have it.

Adam   Well, I would, wouldn't I?

Lia   Where? Where did you meet him?

Adam   Angkor.

A beat.

Lia   I don't believe you.

Adam   Actually, you're right. I might have bumped into him in Sydney first. We didn't get together till Angkor.

Lia   What d'you mean, 'get together'?

Adam   I fucked him.

Lia   Where is he? What happened to him?

Adam   I note the slight shudder at the notion of your son actually fucking someone. Or being fucked, in this instance.

Lia   Where is he?

Adam   It's all very well being liberal and broad-minded, but you don't want to imagine the actual mechanics of it, do you? You can empathise with the world but you don't want its filth on your doorstep. Or, yeeuch! Let's not even go there, in your own bloody drawing room!

Lia   If you've got his stuff you must know where he is.

Adam   There, sadly, I can't help you. I nicked his bag. And I never saw him again.

Lia   You're making this up.

Adam   Which particular bit?

Lia   All of it.

Adam He told me all about you. Writing history books. Nick publishing papers on metaphysical poetry. His grandad. The famous Gordon Kilmartin. You sounded fabulous. You sounded too good to be true.

Lia You're lying.

Adam Give me an instance of when I've lied to you.

Lia Every single thing you've said.

Adam That's Joanna. She's a sociopath. You want to watch her.

Lia I want you to get out of my house and never come back.

Adam He's got a birthmark on the inside of his thigh. I've kissed it.

Lia Nick will be home in a minute.

Adam I'd like to fuck you too. Then I'd really feel part of the family.

Lia He'll be home any minute.

Adam And then what?

Lia I'd like you to be gone before he gets here.

Adam Why?

Lia Because you're polluting the atmosphere in my house.

Adam Because I fucked your dead son?

Lia *slaps him hard across the face.*

Adam Well, he is dead, isn't he? Why don't you admit it? He's not coming back because he's fucking dead.

Lia Because you killed him?

Adam Oh, stop with the melodrama. I fucked him and I nicked his bag. And I never saw him again.

Lia Why did you come here?

Adam You invited me.

Lia What did you want from us?

Adam A bit of what he had.

Lia What?

Adam I fancied being in the bosom of the family. I could have taken over where Adam left off if you hadn't made such a psychodrama about a borrowed shirt. You let me down.

Lia I want you to go right now.

Adam Hey, don't get so rattled.

Lia Get out!

Adam The thing about Adam was, he fucked anything that moved. Really fucking risky. If he's dead, he had it coming –

Lia *picks up the tennis ball machine and hits him with it across the side of his head. He staggers. She hits him again and he goes down. Blood trickles from his head. She stands over him panting, beginning to cry as* **Nick** *comes in.*

Lia I've killed him. I've killed him . . .

They both stare at **Adam** *in horror. He shifts on the floor and raises himself on one elbow.*

Adam You stupid bitch.

Blackout.

Scene Eight

Same room. Later.

Lia *and* **Nick** *are sitting cross-legged on the floor.*

Lia I only took him in because I wanted to be charitable. I wanted to do something good.

Nick You did do good.

Lia I almost killed him.

Nick   Some people are irredeemable.

Lia   I tasted blood in my mouth. When I hit him I wanted him to die. And then I wanted to go on hitting him until he was pulp. I wanted to obliterate his face and wipe him from the face of the earth. There's a murderer inside me.

Nick   He's damaged. He's mad. Madness is terrifying.

Lia   There's no arguing with it. There's no reasoning. It won't be placated by threats, or persuasion or bribes. You can shovel in love and understanding and patience and care, but it's a bottomless pit.

Nick   I think he wanted us to love him.

Lia   He's not loveable.

Nick   He wanted to be Adam.

Lia   Did he have an affair with him?

Nick   He met him and he stole his bag. That's all we'll ever know.

Lia   I've changed the locks.

Nick   He won't come back. He'll go and start again, with new people. Who don't know what he's like. He lives from moment to moment. This lie, that lie, the consequences of the last lie.

Lia   Each one draped in another, in case the light gets through.

Nick   He thinks the truth is whatever comes out of his mouth

Lia   Joyce says she keeps getting his mother on the other side. Who says he's dangerous.

Nick   Joyce would say that.

Lia   Joyce hasn't really got the answers, has she?

Nick   No.

Lia   Some things she says are true. But none of it helps. None of it makes any difference.

Pause.

When Frances Hewer went native and sat in a mud hut for ten years, what d'you think she was trying to do?

Nick   She was in grief.

Lia   I thought all the time that she had the answer. She tried to embrace peace and enlightenment because the alternative was murderous rage. I thought she'd found transcendence.

Nick   Hadn't she?

Lia   Possibly. It's a nice thought. But I'm not convinced. You know what? There is no transcendence, and there are no consolations. Not of religion, or good works, or small acts of charity. Nothing will console us, or help us through this. No good will come of it. There is nothing to be learned. We think our lives are shaped like stories. And stories have endings. Resolutions. But that is not true. Our son is not coming back. Nothing we do will assuage that fact. Ever. I've been seeking consolation where there is none.

Nick   Is it possible to live without consolation?

Lia   Do we have any choice?

Nick   There are small things that console.

Lia   No. Small things will make us fleetingly happy. We'll know moments of joy. Sometimes we'll even forget about it for a while. But we have to live with this hard, metallic truth. He's not coming back. To pretend there's a reason for it, or rosy wisdom to be gained, is to live a lie. Even if we discovered the truth and they found his killers and they were brought to trial. Even if justice were seen to be done. How would that be a consolation?

Nick   It's too bleak.

Lia   I don't think so. I've shed something. False hope. Wanting the past to be different. That desperate search for meaning. I'm looking at it stripped of everything except what it is.

Pause.

I can go on now

Nick   Yes. We'll go on. What else can we do?

Pause.

Lia   But this is the hopeless thing. I still can't say the actual words.

Nick   What words?

Lia   I still can't say 'Adam is dead'.

Nick   So don't.

Lia   Will we ever be one hundred per cent certain?

Nick   I suppose eventually.

Lia   Something happened. A whole series of things. Fleeting connections, accidental links, worlds overlapping, cultures colliding. The wrong place, the wrong time, the wrong choice. We'll never know what they were.

The phone rings. They both tense. **Lia** *looks at* **Nick**.

Lia   Don't answer it.

The phone keeps ringing.

It won't be him.

The phone keeps ringing. They both look at it for a long time. **Lia** *can bear it no longer. She jumps up and grabs the phone.*

Hello?

Fade down lights.